T0376416

Reimagining the *Ballet des Porcelaines*

Reimagining the
BALLET DES PORCELAINES

*A Tale of Magic, Desire,
and Exotic Entanglement*

EDITED BY MEREDITH MARTIN

HARVEY MILLER PUBLISHERS

Reimagining the *Ballet des Porcelaines*

Edited by Meredith Martin,
with contributions by Phil Chan, Christine Jones,
and Charlotte Vignon

HARVEY MILLER PUBLISHERS
An Imprint of Brepols Publishers
London/Turnhout

British Library Cataloguing in Publication Data
A catalogue record for this book
is available from the British Library

ISBN 978-1-912554-81-2
D/2022/0095/98

Designed by Paul van Calster

Printed in the EU on acid-free paper.

The *Ballet des Porcelaines* cast in the Venetian Room, Albertine
Headquarters, Cultural Services of the French Embassy, NYC.
Photographs by Joe Carrotta,
December 2021: pages 52–53, 90–91, 96–97, 113, 156–57.

Performance of the Ballet des Porcelaines in The Carroll and
Milton Petrie European Sculpture Court at The Metropolitan
Museum of Art. Photographs by Joe Carrotta,
December 6, 2021: pages 130–31.

Prince Daniel Applebaum
Princess Georgina Pazcoguin
Sorcerer Tyler Hanes

Contents

MEREDITH MARTIN

Preface and Acknowledgments

In 2016, Charlotte Vignon, then a curator of decorative arts at The Frick Collection in New York, invited me to give a lecture for her exhibition *Porcelain, No Simple Matter: Arlene Shechet and the Arnhold Collection*. It juxtaposed Shechet's contemporary sculptures, made during a residency at the Meissen porcelain manufactory outside of Dresden, with eighteenth-century Meissen objects from the Henry Arnhold collection. Charlotte asked me to contextualize the display in relation to the historical phenomenon of the "porcelain room." In preparing for my talk, I was struck by the myriad ways that Shechet's sculptures and the installation design conveyed the magic and mystery of eighteenth-century porcelain, making it come alive for contemporary audiences. I wondered if I myself could embark on a related creative project, one that departed from the scholar's traditional purview.

Around the same time, my friend Esther Bell told me about a manuscript she had seen at the Bibliothèque nationale de France. It contained the libretto and score for a French pantomime ballet known as the *Ballet des Porcelaines* (and also as *The Teapot Prince*), which had been performed in 1739 and 1741, then lost to the dustbin of history. On my next research trip to Paris, I dug up the manuscript and marveled at its tale of a sorcerer who turns the inhabitants and trespassers of an island he rules into porcelain. The ballet's opening scene of two dancers spinning around until they transformed into porcelain vases enchanted me (I even dreamed about it), and I became obsessed with the idea of resurrecting this lost work—which, like *Sleeping Beauty*, had been slumbering in a box in the archives for nearly three centuries. But as an interloper in the dance world, I had no idea how to do this, and so I applied for and fortunately received a fellowship from New York University's Center for Ballet and the Arts. Everyone at the CBA—especially Jennifer Homans, Andrea Salvatore, Courtney Sams, Christen Douresseau, and the members of my 2020–21 fellowship cohort—was very enthusiastic and supportive of the project. They introduced me to several former fellows who also lent their time and expertise, among them Juliet Bellow, Marina Harss, Hannah Schneider, Catherine Turocy, Heather Ware, and especially Patricia Beaman. Patricia later signed on as our baroque dance specialist.

Through the CBA, I heard about a Zoom lecture that Phil Chan was giving on the history of Orientalism in ballet as it pertained to his activist work as co-founder (with Georgina Pazcoguin) of the organization Final Bow for Yellowface. We all know what Zoom fatigue in the Covid era feels like, but I am so grateful that I pushed through and attended Phil's talk, because it became instantly clear to me that he would be the ideal collaborator and choreographer for reimagining the *Ballet des Porcelaines*. Although I had been focused on conveying the magic and mystery of eighteenth-century porcelain to contemporary audiences, I realized it was also imperative to confront the ballet's problematic *chinoiserie* subtext—its complicity in creating racialized stereotypes of Asian characters that would persist in both ballet and popular culture for centuries to come.

Right after Phil finished his lecture, I cold-emailed him, and despite being involved in many other projects, he agreed to partner with me, which says something about his extraordinary curiosity and open-mindedness. Phil knew right away the mostly Asian-American dream team of dancers and artists he wanted to work with—Georgina Pazcoguin (Princess), Daniel Applebaum (Prince), Tyler Hanes (Sorcerer), Harriet Jung, Sugar Vendil, and Xin Ying—and as soon as he texted them, they too agreed to come on board. (Through Patricia Beaman, we met our wonderful co-musical directors, Dongsok Shin and Leah Gale Nelson.) I am thankful every day that I have had the good fortune to work with Phil, whose creativity and insight into how we, as scholars and artists, make history meaningful for the present have profoundly shaped my thinking in countless ways.

Once we had hashed out the basic parameters of the project, which Phil describes in detail in his essay for this volume, we reached out to our second dream team of museums (many with fabulous porcelain collections) and universities whom we wanted to host performances. Many of them said yes right off the bat, and we are so grateful for their enthusiastic support and input in putting a unique, site-specific spin on each venue. We are also grateful to the representatives of these venues who agreed to write a short essay for the concluding section of this book.

The Museum and Royal Park of Capodimonte, together with the Center for the Art and Architectural History of Port Cities (La Capraia) in Naples, was a key early sponsor, and they helped us make a gorgeous brochure that we used to entice other institutions. (We thank Sylvain Bellenger, Sarah K. Kozlowski, Francesca Santamaria, Francesca Dal Lago, and their colleagues at Capodimonte and La Capraia for this critical support.) Soon after, Wolf Burchard at The Metropolitan Museum of Art in New York became excited about having a performance coincide with the opening of *Inspiring Walt Disney: The Animation of French Decorative Arts*, a major exhibition he was curating, and he convinced his colleagues to host our world premiere. We are so grateful to Wolf, Sarah Lawrence, Maeve Dare, and everyone at The Met who made this possible.

My dear friend Charlotte Vignon, who is now director of the National Museum of Ceramics at Sèvres, has been a vital supporter and collaborator from the beginning, and we are grateful to her and her colleagues at Sèvres, particularly Romane Sarfati. Mia Jackson at Waddesdon was an early champion, and her ideas about programming, particularly for schoolchildren, helped shape the project. We thank Mia and her colleagues, among them Sarah Dewberry and Pippa Shirley, as well as Leona Forsyth and the Rothschild Foundation for her guidance and its generous support. We also thank Kate Tunstall at Oxford, who is organizing a related symposium and made it possible for us to receive funding from TORCH | The Oxford Research Centre in the Humanities as well as from the British Society for Eighteenth-Century Studies (BSECS). We owe a debt of gratitude to everyone involved in these endeavors, in particular Liz Green and Krisztina Lugosi from TORCH as well as our UK-based period instrument ensemble, Instruments of Time & Truth.

After Kee Il Choi invited me to speak about the project in his "Global Interchange" seminar, Hedley Swain, director of the Royal Pavilion & Museums Trust, Brighton & Hove, contacted us about bringing the ballet there. We are thrilled to be performing in the Royal Pavilion's spectacular Music Room and are grateful to Hedley and his colleagues, especially Alexandra Loske, Caroline Sutton, and Charlotte Desjarlais. We also thank Bruno Racine, director of the Palazzo Grassi (whom we met through the Capodimonte team), as well as his colleagues Francesca Colasante, Suzel Berneron, Jacqueline Feldmann, and Mauro Baronchelli, for hosting us on the magical island of Venice.

Simon Morrison, a leading music historian, kindly shared his experience with reviving ballets and suggested I bring the project to Princeton, where he teaches. His colleagues Wendy Heller, chair of the music department, and Tina Fehlandt of the dance department have helped make this happen, and we are grateful to them as well as to Elizabeth Rouget, Wendy Young, Bridget Alsdorf, Andrea Immel, Anne Cheng, and everyone else who has been involved there. Similarly, Judith Zeitlin has been instrumental in bringing the ballet to the University of Chicago and creating robust programming around it, particularly in partnership with the Smart Museum of Art. We owe huge thanks to Judith as well as to Craig Trompeter of the Haymarket Opera Company, Wu Hung, Martha Feldman, Orianna Cacchione, Abbey Newman, Connie Yip, and Julia Rhoads. Although we planned it too late for them to be included in this book, Jeff Ravel and Kristel Smentek have arranged for us to bring the ballet to the Massachusetts Institute of Technology in September 2022. We are also grateful to Graham Lustig, Bat Abbit, and the Oakland Ballet Company for taking on the production beginning in autumn 2022, allowing it to have a continued life in their active repertory and educational programs. We are delighted and humbled that so many terrific organizations have signed on to the project and we thank every person involved—many more than we can name, and some of whom we met after this volume went to press.

We must also express our deep thanks to the Arnhold Family Foundation, especially Jody, Paul, and Julia Arnhold, for generously supporting the ballet's creation, which honors Jody Arnhold's commitment to dance as well as her father-in-law Henry Arnhold's superb porcelain collection. In addition, we are grateful to New York University—in particular the Department of Art History, the College of Arts and Sciences, and the Provost's Global Research Initiative—for supporting both the ballet and this book, and for providing invaluable technical and administrative assistance. Special thanks go to Margaret Coon, Akeem Flavors, Jair Kessler, Maya Jex, and Carolyn Dinshaw. The European Commission has also provided funding and has enabled Elisa Cazzato, a specialist in eighteenth-century stage design, to take part in the project.

Many institutions and individuals have invited us to speak about the *Ballet des Porcelaines* and have shared their insight along the way. In addition to those cited above, we thank Lisa Freeman and David Taylor from the R18 Collective; Ellen Welch and Amanda Moehlenpah from The University of North Carolina at Chapel Hill; Pauline Chevalier from the Institute national d'histoire de l'art; Charlotte Guichard from the École normale supérieure; and Caite Panzer and her team from the Cultural Services of the French Embassy for organizing a fabulous photo shoot and event on our behalf. For either contributing to the book or for providing critical feedback, research, photographs, proofreading, and moral support, we owe huge thanks to Noelle Barr, Joy Cador, Joe Carrotta, Jeffrey Collins, Mim Harrison, Tav Holmes, Christine Jones, Anna Kisselgoff, Anna Sujin Leckie, David Pullins, Dominique Quéro, Mei Mei Rado, Geoffrey Ripert, Cynthia Volk, and Chi-ming Yang.

Finally, I am so grateful to have had the opportunity to work again with the brilliant and exceedingly patient editor Johan Van der Beke and his team at Harvey Miller and Brepols, especially Alexandra Hoare, Paul van Calster, and Quinten Vervecken.

Contributors

PATRICIA BEAMAN, baroque dance consultant for the *Ballet des Porcelaines*, began her journey in baroque dance with the New York Baroque Dance Company. She is a faculty member of Wesleyan Dance and New York University's Open Arts program, and is the author of *World Dance Cultures: From Ritual to Spectacle* (2018).

SYLVAIN BELLENGER is Director of the Museo e Real Bosco di Capodimonte in Naples.

WOLF BURCHARD is Associate Curator in the European Sculpture and Decorative Arts Department at The Metropolitan Museum of Art, New York. He is the curator of *Inspiring Walt Disney: The Animation of French Decorative Arts* (2021) and author of *The Sovereign Artist: Charles Le Brun and the Image of Louis XIV* (2016).

PHIL CHAN, co-creator and choreographer, is the co-founder of Final Bow for Yellowface (www.yellowface.org), which addresses outdated portrayals of Asians on the performing arts stages. He is also the author of *Final Bow for Yellowface: Dancing between Intention and Impact* (2020).

MIA JACKSON is Curator of Decorative Arts at Waddesdon Manor. She previously worked in the Prints and Drawings Department at The British Museum, The Wallace Collection, and English Heritage. She is currently preparing a series of exhibitions on Alice de Rothschild with her Waddesdon colleagues.

CHRISTINE JONES is Assistant Director for Academic Affairs in University Honors and Affiliate Professor of French at the University of Maryland, College Park. She is the translator of *Mother Goose Refigured: A Critical Translation of Charles Perrault's Fairy Tales* (2016) and author of *Shapely Bodies: The Image of Porcelain in Eighteenth-Century France* (2013).

HARRIET JUNG is a Korean American costume designer working primarily in dance. She is the co-founder of Reid & Harriet, along with Reid Bartelme.

SARAH K. KOZLOWSKI is Associate Director of the Edith O'Donnell Institute of Art History at the University of Texas at Dallas, and Director of the Centro per la Storia dell'Arte e dell'Architettura delle Città Portuali, La Capraia.

ALEXANDRA LOSKE is a German British art historian, writer, and curator with a particular interest in late eighteenth- and early nineteenth-century art and architecture. She is a curator at the Royal Pavilion & Museums Trust, Brighton & Hove, and has published and lectured widely on color history and other subjects.

MEREDITH MARTIN, co-creator and producer, is Associate Professor of Art History at New York University. A specialist in early modern French art, she is the author of *Dairy Queens: The Politics of Pastoral Architecture from Catherine de' Medici to Marie-Antoinette* (2012) and *The Sun King at Sea: Maritime Art and Galley Slavery in Louis XIV's France* (2022; co-authored with Gillian Weiss).

LEAH GALE NELSON, baroque violinist and co-musical director, is a performer-educator in the field of historical performance, and a visiting scholar at Rutgers University. She is a curator of historical projects, including a recording titled *Biber: The Sacred Mysteries* and a reprise of her retro-hp ensemble, *LOUIS LOUIS*, for the *Ballet des Porcelaines*.

BRUNO RACINE is Director of Palazzo Grassi and was formerly Chief Executive of the Pompidou Center and of the Bibliothèque nationale de France in Paris.

ELIZABETH ROUGET is a PhD candidate in Musicology at Princeton University, where she is specializing in seventeenth- and eighteenth-century baroque opera and ballet. Her interests include the transatlantic export of European dance knowledge into the culture of American colonies.

ROMANE SARFATI is CEO of the Manufacture et musées nationaux of Sèvres and Limoges. She was formerly in the public service at Musée du quai Branly, City of Paris, and in the Ministry of Culture Cabinet as counselor in charge of visual arts, architecture, design, fashion, and crafts.

KATE TUNSTALL is Professor of French at the University of Oxford, and Tutorial Fellow of Worcester College. Her research focuses primarily on the French literature of the eighteenth century and on Denis Diderot, in particular; with Katie Scott she translated Diderot's *Regrets sur ma vieille robe de chambre* (2016).

SUGAR VENDIL, *kintsugi* music creator, is a composer, pianist, and interdisciplinary artist based in New York. Her work is introspective, ruminating on memory and experience.

CHARLOTTE VIGNON is Director of the National Museum of Ceramics at Sèvres and former curator of decorative arts at The Frick Collection in New York, where she curated the 2016 exhibition *Porcelain, No Simple Matter: Arlene Shechet and the Arnhold Collection*.

XIN YING, assistant choreographer and dancer, is a principal with the Martha Graham Dance Company. She was the director of the Dance Department at Sichuan College of Arts & Culture and a guest teacher at the Graham School, the Beijing Dance Academy, and Nanjing University of Arts.

JUDITH T. ZEITLIN is William R. Kenan, Jr. Professor in East Asian Languages and Civilizations at the University of Chicago. Her many publications include *Performing Images: Opera in Chinese Visual Culture*, co-edited with Yuhang Li (2014). She is currently collaborating with composer Yao Chen on the creation of the opera *Ghost Village*, for which she has written the libretto.

I

Historical Reimaginings

I

Historical Reimaginings

MEREDITH MARTIN

ONCE UPON A TIME AT THE CHÂTEAU DE MORVILLE

Commerce, Colonialism, and Chinoiserie in the Ballet des Porcelaines

≈ For Mary Sheriff

In September 1739, a group of French aristocrats gathered at the château de Morville, a country house about thirty-five miles from Paris. Among them were the widow of Charles-Jean-Baptiste Fleuriau, comte de Morville (1686–1732), the estate's former owner, and their adult children; Jean Jacques Amelot de Chaillou, France's secretary of state for foreign affairs; Charles-Antoine Coypel, who served as first painter (*premier peintre*) to King Louis XV (1710–1774; r. 1715–74); and Anne Claude de Tubières-Grimoard de Pestels de Lévis, comte de Caylus (1692–1765), a noted author, scholar, and collector. Together they comprised an elite *théâtre de société*: a private, mostly amateur theater troupe that staged dances and plays for their own amusement. Assembled in the late 1720s, the Morville society performed on and off for about fifteen years, and their heyday at this château occurred between 1737 and 1741.[1]

On the night of September 20, the group staged a one-act comedy by Caylus on the theme of love's vicissitudes, followed by a short divertissement in the form of a pantomime ballet entitled *The Teapot Prince* (*Le Prince Pot-à-Thé*), also known as the *Ballet des Porcelaines*. Likewise written by Caylus, with music by Nicolas-Racot de Grandval (1676–1753), and based on the fairy tale *Prince Perinet, or the Origin of Pagodes* (1731), it tells the story of a prince and princess stranded on an exotic island ruled by an evil sorcerer, who has transformed its inhabitants into porcelain. Separated from his beloved, the prince is turned into a teapot, and he suffers this fate until the princess, in a reversal of the standard damsel-in-distress plot, seduces the sorcerer, steals his wand, and breaks the spell, bringing everyone back to life. In the fairy tale, the sorcerer is punished by being turned into a pagod—a small porcelain figure based on Chinese *Budai* sculptures that were popular in Europe at the time—but in the ballet he simply flees the stage. At the end, the couple reunites and the cast, which included household servants dressed in cardboard costumes to imitate the island's porcelain captives, reassemble to perform a contredanse. The entire production, Caylus wrote, was meant to last "no more than a generous fifteen minutes."[2]

Aside from the libretto and the score, nothing survives of the *Ballet des Porcelaines*, and it appears to have been performed only twice at the château de Morville—in September 1739 and June 1741—and nowhere since. Neither the full libretto nor the score was published prior to the late twentieth century, and no one seems to have commented on the production at the time.[3] Nonetheless, aspects of the ballet resound in later works by the troupe and its associates, including Gabrielle-Suzanne Barbot de Villeneuve's *Beauty and the Beast* (1740). It also prefigured later pantomime ballets like Jean-Georges Noverre's *Les Fêtes Chinoises* (c. 1751), which portrays "Chinese" dancers who metamorphose into porcelain vases.[4] Moreover, there is evidence that the *Ballet des Porcelaines* was known to the French Russian choreographer Marius Petipa and may have inspired his collaborations with Pyotr Ilych Tchaikovsky, including an intermezzo with dancing porcelain statues that Petipa choreographed for *The Queen of Spades* (1890).[5] So despite its obscurity, the *Ballet des Porcelaines* seems to have had a vibrant afterlife, reemerging even in such iconic productions as *The Nutcracker*, *Sleeping Beauty*, and *Beauty and the Beast*.

A prologue written for the ballet's 1741 performance—in which members of the Morville troupe bemoan the "cruel torment" of having to wait nearly two years to restage it—provides some information about the *mise-en-scène*.[6] On that occasion, according to the prologue, the ballet was performed in the château's gardens, at night, in front of an illuminated water feature surrounded by porcelain vases (or, more likely, cardboard imitations of porcelain vases) and framed by a lit archway with a teapot underneath. Albeit on a more intimate scale, the description calls to mind a royal fête staged in the gardens of Versailles in July 1668 as depicted in an engraving by Jean Lepautre (Fig. 2). Organized to glorify Louis XIV's purportedly "limitless" reach and to honor his new mistress, Madame de Montespan, the fête included as part of its décor scores of ceramic vessels that anticipated the legendary *Trianon de porcelaine* erected two years later in the gardens.[7] At both Versailles and Morville, porcelain evoked not only the faraway realms of China and Japan but also France's desire to bring Asian luxury goods closer to home, especially porcelain, the quasi-mystical substance that Europeans had for centuries tried (and failed) to make. That desire also formed the subtext to Caylus's ballet, and in the 1741 prologue it was encapsulated in a scene in which the prince, who was probably played by Morville's son, sailed across the water in a small boat, conjuring the theme of island transport but also the many vessels bringing Chinese and Japanese treasures to France.[8]

Ships, porcelain, visions of enchantment in exotic lands: all of these motifs were familiar to members of the Morville coterie. The comte de Morville's parents had been ardent collectors of Asian porcelain, lacquer, and other goods, and they had heavily invested in merchant vessels operated by France's Compagnie de la Chine and Compagnie des Indes.[9] A few decades earlier, they had hired the Parisian artist Claude Audran III to design a *cabinet chinois* for their newly acquired château de la Muette, a commission that Audran passed on to his assistant, Antoine Watteau.[10] Watteau's designs as well as engravings made after them spurred a craze for what would retrospectively be termed *chinoiserie*—a global decorative style inspired by images, materials, and ideas of China that was in full swing by the time the ballet was performed.[11] The comte de Morville inherited both his family's love of porcelain and his father's appointments as naval minister and secretary of state for foreign affairs, meaning that he oversaw French policies related to global commerce. Members of his troupe had similar high-level connections, and they too were avid consumers of Asian wares. In addition to collecting porcelain, the comte de Caylus wrote Orientalist fairy tales, while his brother Charles undertook naval missions in the Mediterranean prior to becoming governor of France's West Indian colonies of Martinique and Guadeloupe. In short, the group had multiple

Illuminations du Palais et des Jardins de Versailles

V.

Nocturnæ Jlluminationes, vasis statuisque incluso igne pellucentibus, ad Palatij Versaliani fenestras, et per omnes hortorum areas et xystos aptè dispositis.

le Pautre sculps. 1679.

FIGURE 2

Jean Lepautre, "Illuminations of the Palace and Gardens of Versailles," from André Félibien, *Relation de la fête de Versailles du 18 juillet 1668* (Paris: de l'Imprimerie royale, 1679). Etching and engraving, 30.1 × 41.8 cm. British Museum, London. © The Trustees of the British Museum.

frames of reference for the *Ballet des Porcelaines* and would no doubt have viewed it in both aesthetic and political terms—which, as we will see, were closely linked.

This essay draws on a range of sources—archival documents, porcelain figures, dance diagrams, maps, and fairy tales—to imagine what the *Ballet des Porcelaines* might have looked like and how it might have been interpreted by its eighteenth-century performers and audiences. I aim to reconstruct both a "period eye" and a "period body" for this production, taking into account not only the French bodies of the Morville clan but also the Asian "others" they were claiming to incarnate. Much of the scholarship on early modern French ballet, luxury consumption, and *chinoiserie* has focused on the role that such practices played in shaping elite identity at home: in reconfiguring class distinctions, for example, or in providing a flexible form of masquerade through which Europeans could mobilize and express new forms of self. Less has been said about how these purportedly frivolous pastimes also helped shape ideas about the other that would play a vital, and devastating, role in developing racial theories and in geopolitics.[12] In the case of the *Ballet des Porcelaines*, the pleasure and empowerment it conferred on the Morville clan came at the cost of belittling the other, whose own personhood was denied or transformed into trivial ornament.[13] I explore this process as it materialized in the ballet

A collection of fanciful French masquerade attire from around 1725 includes a costume for a pagod that suggests what these "grotesque" performers might have looked like (Fig. 4). Attributed to Jean II Bérain or his circle, the drawing depicts a figure squatting with crossed arms and legs on a tasseled green pillow, dressed in a pink and white "Chinese" dressing gown with a conical hat on his head.[24] The exoticism of his dress complements the strange, feline otherness of his features, especially his whisker-like beard and the shape of his eyes. Even stranger is the accompanying description of his movements, which indicates that his crossed legs were fake and that he was meant to stand inside the pedestal to which he was attached via straps on his belt, like a human jack-in-the-box. As the performer walked or leaped, his pedestal would move with him, adding to the comic effect but also to the conceit of an inanimate object coming to life—or, conversely, of a person becoming a thing. For those who witnessed such a performance, it must have lingered in their minds when later encountering pagods in Parisian shops and residences, where these figures would often be fitted with bronze mounts or attached to candelabra and other *objets d'art*—gilded "cages" from which one could imagine them arising and starting to dance (see Fig. 18).[25]

A third masquerade held at Versailles in 1700 was hosted by the wife of Louis Phélypeaux de Pontchartrain, France's naval minister who had green-lit the *Amphitrite* mission. Madame de Pontchartrain scored a coup in getting the duchesse de Bourgogne, future mother of Louis XV, to attend, dressed in a Chinese costume that her Jesuit confessor Louis Le Comte (the same Le Comte who wrote about China) had helped her devise. Her husband, Louis XIV's grandson, attended yet another fête dressed by Bérain as a Chinese sorcerer or "druid," complete with a long beard, a conical hat, and a diamond-patterned cape (Fig. 5). His outfit recalled the *commedia dell'arte* character Harlequin, who sometimes performed as a talking Chinese pagod, and who often appeared in blackface to signify his "lowly" origins and "devilish" nature, attributes that likely contributed to emerging racial stereotypes.[26] All of these performances spoke to the ways in which "China" and its products could be transformed into a playful, malleable object for European self-definition: one that enabled former members of the merchant class, like the Ponchartrains, to gain access to the upper echelons of court society, or provided a means for royal family members (such as the duc de Bourgogne or his father, the Grand Dauphin) to subvert the classical aesthetics and absolutist politics of the court.[27] But they also conveyed how, with the rise of global consumer capitalism, the very definition of "self" was becoming increasingly reliant on or synonymous with "things"—a conceit that the *Ballet des Porcelaines* would exploit.[28]

Whereas most French elites were enchanted by Asian goods, some claimed that the influx of exotic commodities would damage the economy, ruin native industries, and destroy standards of beauty and taste. For his part, Le Comte wrote that he "wished the designs the Chinese used in painting and porcelain were more beautiful [...] their human figures are all crippled (*estropiées*)."[29] He worried that European viewers would mistake these misshapen forms for the bodies of actual Chinese people, an anxiety that several of his Jesuit colleagues shared.[30] Whether or not this misrecognition occurred—and it seems likely that it did occur, given that artists like François Boucher often used pagods (which Boucher collected) as models for human figures in paintings and prints (Fig. 6)—Europeans eagerly procured these figures and replicated them in manufactories they set up at Delft, Meissen, Chantilly, and elsewhere.[31]

Pagods were among the very first objects created at Meissen, the first European manufactory to succeed in making true or hard-paste porcelain, and they continued to be made there throughout the eighteenth and nineteenth centuries. (Meissen was founded around 1710 by the ruler of Saxony, Augustus the Strong, who was so fanatical about Asian porcelain that he once traded six hundred of his cavalrymen to the king of Prussia in exchange for 151 blue-and-white Ming vases—a perverse example of the eighteenth-century interchangeability between persons and things.)[32] Over time, these European pagods deviated from faithful imitations of Chinese *Budai* figures and acquired exaggerated, grotesque features like wide, lipstick grins, fawning postures, or, in the case of "nodding" types, moveable hands, necks, and tongues (Fig. 7). Although some *Budai* and *Guanyin* figures were also made with detachable heads for greater ease of production and transport, these modifications added to the doll- or puppet-like nature of European pagods and made them appear more childish and ridiculous—qualities that the French writer Denis Diderot would later attribute to Chinese people as well as to French consumers obsessed with these "precious knick-knacks" (*colifichets précieux*) to the detriment of "the nation" as a whole.[33] Diderot, along with the comte de Caylus, also bemoaned the impact that the proliferation of pagods in elite interiors was having on French depictions of the human body. In a 1749 lecture to the Royal Academy, Caylus argued that these figurines should be replaced by "good models" and "beautiful bronzes" that he felt would better serve its students. At the same time, he amassed a cache of more than eighty pagods to adorn his private residence.[34]

French artisans at Chantilly, a porcelain manufactory founded in 1726 by the prince de Condé, likewise amplified stereotypically "grotesque" features of their pagods, giving them toothy grins, elongated heads, facial hair, and, in some cases, dark skin, a modification also evident in a series of blackface, pipe-smoking pagods made at Delft in the late seventeenth century. The Delft figures reveal how portrayals of Chinese peoples were sometimes conflated with images of enslaved Africans, particularly those forcibly transported to the West (rather than East) Indies to produce tobacco for European consumption.[35] Around this same time, the French physician and traveler François Bernier, to whom the modern understanding of "race" is often attributed, attempted in a 1684 essay to classify different "species" of human beings from around the world based on physiognomy and skin color. One wonders to what extent Bernier's ideas were mediated through his encounter with art objects, particularly with respect to China, where so little actual contact with Europeans occurred. Although Bernier, along with many of his contemporaries, described the skin color of East Asians as "truly white" (like the porcelain they produced), his recounting of their features—"broad shoulders, flat faces, small hidden noses, little, long, and deep-set pig's eyes, three hairs of a beard"—is echoed in a Chantilly pagod representing the Daoist deity Shoulao from around 1735–40 (Fig. 8). Although the pagod's brown skin is not entirely unknown in Chinese depictions of the deity, it was rare, and it indicates how French artisans at this time were both grappling with and constructing new racial categories that were later used to denigrate others.[36]

The racialized associations of some of these figures extended to *magot*, an alternative word for a pagod that, according to the 1694 Academy dictionary, denoted both a "very ugly man" and a type of "Barbary" (North African) monkey.[37] Monkeys and Chinese human bodies were frequently conflated in European *chinoiserie*, and manufacturers at both Meissen and Chantilly sculpted monkey figurines with facial features,

Medecin Chinois

poses, and functions similar to those of pagods and *magots* (Fig. 9). At the château de Chantilly, such porcelain figures would have resonated with the prince de Condé's *Grande Singerie* (Monkey Cabinet), which was probably decorated by Christophe Huet in the late 1730s, contemporaneous with Caylus's ballet.[38] Its walls, which quote Watteau's *cabinet chinois* at La Muette, were painted with representations of Asian men and women (as well as African and Amerindian figures) and with monkeys in Chinese dress, all making music and engaging in playful activities (Fig. 10). To be fair, monkeys also appear in European costume, and the conceit of "aping" extends to both cultures, notably in a vignette that appears to poke fun at the prince's frustrated efforts to replicate true porcelain. Nonetheless, insofar as the room's décor thematizes French aristocratic pursuits and comportment, and seems to lampoon those who fall short of achieving proper "Frenchification" (*francisation*, a term used at the time to denote efforts to "civilize" Indigenous inhabitants of France's New World colonies), there is a difference between the lighthearted self-parody aimed at the prince and his circle and the potentially more insidious caricaturing of foreigners—particularly when such simian imagery would later inform pseudo-scientific theories of race.[39]

The Chantilly *Singerie* has been linked to eighteenth-century fairy tales, including Madame de Villeneuve's *Beauty and the Beast*, and both the prince de Condé and Villeneuve had ties to the Morville clan.[40] *Beauty and the Beast*, like the Orientalist tales by the French writer Madame d'Aulnoy—which feature magical porcelain palaces, monkeys in Chinese costume, and, in one case, an entire "race" of animated porcelain pagods—similarly foregrounds themes of human-animal and human-object transformation in a way that has racial and colonial undertones.[41] For Villeneuve, these motifs were connected to her family's involvement in the transatlantic slave trade, a context referenced in her story's frame narrative (about a young girl who sails from La Rochelle to France's Caribbean colony of Saint-Domingue to marry a plantation owner) and implied in the tale itself. Her protagonist, Belle, is promised to an unruly Beast, who, through love, becomes "Frenchified" and unveils his princely origins. In his enchanted castle, situated in a tropical landscape, Belle is waited on by monkeys (*magots*) and is served colonial beverages like chocolate in (presumably porcelain) cups that seem to materialize and move of their own accord—arguably because the enslaved labor associated with them has been suppressed or erased.[42]

Some of these themes appear in the fairy tale that inspired the *Ballet des Porcelaines*, entitled *Prince Perinet, or the Origin of Pagodes*. Published anonymously in 1731, it may have been written earlier, possibly by the chevalier de Mailly, whose family supported the Caylus clan, had ties to the French navy and the court, and spurred the French craze for *chinoiserie*.[43] Whereas Caylus's bare-bones libretto gives very few details about its characters and setting—most likely because he and his troupe members were already familiar with this tale—*Perinet* is more explicit about its Asian setting and subtext, which is also signified by the presence of porcelain, teapots, and tea. The prince's nemesis, Nortandose, is described as "a genie [or magician] of the strongest sort" and a passionate lover of porcelain; he rules a part of "the Indies" (*les Indes*) known as the Blue Island or the Island of Porcelains, conjuring the blue-and-white Chinese wares that were the first of their kind to be imported en masse into Europe.[44] Nortandose tricks the hapless prince, whose name loosely resembles *peri*, the term for a Persian winged spirit or fairy, into traveling to his island atop a toad,

FIGURE 7

"Nodding" pagod with movable neck and hands, c. 1730–40. Meissen manufactory, hard-paste porcelain, 19 × 19 × 17 cm. Sèvres–Manufacture et musée nationaux, MNC2274–37. Photo © RMN-Grand Palais (Sèvres–Manufacture et musée nationaux) / Martine Beck-Coppola.

FIGURE 8

Shoulao, c. 1735–40. Chantilly manufactory, tin-glazed soft-paste porcelain decorated in polychrome enamels, 26 × 21.9 × 11.4 cm. The Metropolitan Museum of Art, The Jack and Belle Linsky Collection, 1982 (1982.60.371).

FIGURE 9

Johann Joachim Kändler (attr.), Monkey, c. 1740 (after a model of c. 1732). Meissen manufactory, hard-paste porcelain, 24.1 cm. The Metropolitan Museum of Art, The Jack and Belle Linsky Collection, 1982 (1982.60.310).

FIGURE 10

Christophe Huet, Allegory of Asia from the *Grande Singerie*
at Chantilly, late 1730s. Musée Condé, Chantilly.
Photo © RMN-Grand Palais (domaine de Chantilly) / Michel Urtado.

whereupon he turns him into a yellow teapot—the only teapot among the captives and apparently the only yellow vessel on an otherwise "blue" island.

Although we don't know whether these colors were adopted in the original ballet performances, the choice of yellow does not seem accidental, and it reveals France's complex attitudes toward Asian and possibly European rivals in porcelain manufacture. In the 1720s and 1730s, yellow was used as a ground color at the French factory of Saint-Cloud, but it was also a prominent color at Meissen, where it was likely inspired by Chinese yellow-ground porcelains in Augustus the Strong's collection, in addition to being associated with the Saxon Polish court.[45] Both Meissen and Saint-Cloud produced numerous yellow teapots and other wares with Chinese-inspired shapes and motifs, indicating that this hue may have resonated with *Perinet*'s writer or readers as a signifier either for China, Saxony, or Saint-Cloud (Fig. 11). Additionally, whereas most European sources at the time linked the color yellow with the Chinese imperial court, in 1735 Carl Linneaus classified *Homo Asiaticus* as "yellow," setting the stage for later attacks on East Asians as "the yellow race" and as purveyors of yellow "peril" and contagion, which has strong resonances to this day—including in our current Covid-19 pandemic.[46]

Teapots, in turn, were associated with both women and China in Europe, where tea drinking (particularly in Britain) evoked feminine politeness and sociability but also exoticism, overindulgence, and dissipation—themes that are reinforced in the fairy tale. For example, the island's porcelain vessels "madly" dote on Perinet's magical spaniel, incessantly cooing "nonsense" to him, just as the author claims real-life women do with their lap dogs.[47] Such connotations are also apparent in an English porcelain tea caddy from 1745–50 that takes the form of a toothy, open-mouthed pagod (Fig. 12).[48] All of these associations may have been carried over into the ballet's staging and choreography, although Caylus's libretto is missing a crucial plot point: the moment where Perinet, while still a teapot, climbs atop a doorway and flings himself onto the sorcerer's head—thereby smashing into pieces and breaking the spell, while also (with the help of the female protagonists) transforming Nortandose into the first or "original" pagod, complete with a nodding head. In our contemporary reimagining, we have chosen to retain this transformation scene, while also recasting Nortandose as a "mad" European porcelain collector modeled on Meissen's Augustus the Strong. In so doing, we aim to explore the multifaceted politics and rivalries that we see in the work as well as the complex dualities of its characters, who would later become ossified into cultural, racial, and gendered stereotypes that were used in the nineteenth century and afterward to fuel European attacks on China as well as anti-Asian sentiment.

While parodying the eighteenth-century obsession with origins (and the consumer craze for pagods), *Prince Perinet* underscores significant links between fairy tales, scientific inquiry, and the quest for knowledge and possession.[49] Knowledge here seems expressly tied to porcelain manufacture, an alchemical "magic" that Europeans had long been desperate to attain. Whereas chemists at Meissen had finally succeeded in divining the formula, French manufactories at Saint-Cloud, Chantilly, and Vincennes (which was founded around the same time as the ballet) were still jockeying to unveil the mystery, while making desirable soft-paste variants in the meantime. (For more on European porcelain production around 1740, see Charlotte Vignon's essay in this volume.) *Prince Perinet*, as Christine Jones has argued, can be interpreted as an allegory of the French desire to know and seize the secrets of porcelain manufacture, so as to "beat the Chinese at their craft" and reap the financial and aesthetic benefits of making and selling their own porcelain wares.[50] But the tale could also be read more broadly as a power play, one that ends with the liberation of French consumers from the imprisoning sway of Asian and rival European commodities (as personified by the yellow tea-pot), and with the diminution of a formerly fearsome China into an absurd pagod.

In both *Perinet* and the *Ballet des Porcelaines*, this victory is secured through the transformative power of love—the "sole enchanter," according to a refrain sung at the ballet's outset (see Fig. 56). French artworks at the time populated China not only with grotesque pagods but also with amorous couples and alluring young women who resembled their European counterparts in pastoral paintings by Watteau and Boucher. Watteau's designs for the *cabinet chinois* portray beautiful, rosy-cheeked

FIGURE 12

Tea caddy in the form of a pagod, 1745–50. Chelsea manufactory, soft-paste porcelain, 17.1 x 11.4 cm. The Metropolitan Museum of Art, Gift of Irwin Untermeyer, 1964 (64.101.415a, b).

FIGURE 13

Antoine Watteau, *Chinese Woman of Koeui Tchéou*, painting for the *cabinet chinois* at La Muette, c. 1710. Oil on canvas, 23.4 x 18.2 cm. Private Collection. Image courtesy of Koetser Gallery, Zurich.

"Chinese" women, including one from the province of "Koeui Tchéou" (Fig. 13), who look more than a little like French shepherdesses, while in his libretto Caylus states that the prince could be dressed either in royal garb or as a shepherd, "depending on the costume available." While this conflation of the pastoral with *chinoiserie* might seem odd, it constituted another way in which French artists expressed a longing for China and its products: via the seductive language of *galanterie*. Defined as a "gendered model of communication and sociability between sexes," *galanterie* also became, according to Charlotte Guichard, a model for French commercial and colonial relations, one that had its apotheosis on stage in Jean-Philippe Rameau's 1735 opera-ballet *Les Indes galantes*.[51] At the same time, by linking China to the pastoral mode (as Gherardini did in his account), eighteenth-century French artists helped shape an image of temporal and developmental distance that inverted earlier accounts of China's advanced civilization by reframing it as a primitive Arcadia. All of these poles—the *galant* and the grotesque, the beautiful and the ugly, the civilized and the "savage"—coexisted in the ballet and in visions of the East associated with the Morville society, to whom we now turn.

Act I The Comte de Morville and the Caylus Brothers: Commerce, Culture, and Colonialism

The comte de Morville grew up surrounded by what Katie Scott has described as "the d'Armenonville passion for things Oriental." His family's Parisian residence on the rue Platrière held an abundance of Asian porcelain and other wares, including Chinese blue-and-white plates, Japanese vases, a silver-mounted tea set, and, in a gallery on the first floor, a pair of two-foot-high pagods (possibly of wood), "each holding a child."[52] These objects were integrated into an interior that, despite period admonitions not to make one's home look "like a dealer's shop,"[53] advertised the family's investment in the Asia trade. Lacquer cabinets, Persian carpets, *toiles indiennes*, and Chinese screens competed for attention, while in the garden, a white marble statue of the sea goddess Amphitrite alluded to the ship that brought Asian goods to France.[54] At the family's château de La Muette, these treasures were complemented by Watteau's *cabinet chinois*, where guests were transported to the artist's vision of China as a lush fairy land at once familiar and strange: filled with life-sized vases, oneiric topography, and pagod-like men of an "irreducible otherness," but also with charming women, children, and families.[55] Although the room was probably dismantled in the late 1730s, Watteau's designs circulated widely as prints beginning in 1731 and gave rise to the style that would come to be known as *chinoiserie*. The *cabinet chinois* must have had some impact on the conceptualization and aesthetic of the *Ballet des Porcelaines*, and in our production, Phil Chan invokes it by choreographing a closing tableau for the dancers inspired by one of these prints (Fig. 14).

During the first quarter of the eighteenth century, France's trade with Asia continued to underperform relative to the more powerful Dutch and British East India companies, and many *marchands merciers*, including Watteau's dealer Edmé-François Gersaint, satisfied their clients' taste for Asian wares by buying them through these corporations.[56] Morville himself probably obtained porcelain this way, especially after he was named ambassador to the Netherlands in 1718. While residing in Holland, he and his wife bought art for themselves and their friends, including France's Regent.[57] In 1722 he was promoted to naval minister, and in 1723 to secretary of state for foreign affairs. His duties included directing the movements and activities of

Idole de la Déesse KI MÂO SÁO dans le Royaume de Mang au pays des Laos

Tiré du Cabinet du Roy au Château de la Meute
à Paris avec Privilège.

French ambassadors throughout Europe as well as contracting with jewelers and merchants to create royal gifts, which is how he may have first encountered purveyors of exotic luxury goods.[58] He also oversaw the regulation of Asian imports and raw materials brought via the Dutch East India Company into France, and he fielded requests from French shippers who, hoping to vie with European rivals for the China trade, asked the Crown to waive transport fees and other "obstructions" that were "prejudicial to commerce."[59]

Morville's role as stage manager for France's international trade is acknowledged in a travel account first published in 1725 (and then reprinted multiple times over the next decade) entitled *Nouveau voyage autour du monde*. It was written by Jean-Baptiste Le Gentil de La Barbinais, a French trader and (allegedly) the first French circumnavigator, who took the longer Pacific Ocean route to China favored by some French seafarers that included stopovers at South American ports in Chile and Peru. Le Gentil's tome features a frontispiece engraved by Louis Audran, a relative of Watteau's teacher, and nautical charts showing distant lands, among them the Peruvian port of Ylo being approached by European ships (Fig. 15). Loosely resembling dance diagrams of the period—with ships in place of dancers' bodies and feet (see Fig. 20)—their bird's-eye perspective, dynamic rhumb lines, and arabesque flourishes visually echo the author's recounting of his comprehensive movements and commanding grasp of these foreign territories—a confidence that belies the fact that he returned home empty-handed and bankrupt.

Le Gentil dedicated his tome to Morville, and here he is more modest, gallantly thanking the minister for not having "spurned the homage that my heart hastens to pay you." Financial failure aside, the *Nouveau Voyage* is notable for its detailed descriptions of China and Chinese people, whom the author praises in many respects, while also acknowledging that many of their customs seem "bizarre" and "barbaric." Seemingly acknowledging while also dismissing earlier, more deferential accounts, he writes, "I esteem the Chinese, but this esteem does not blind me to the point of considering them superior to us. You will know by what follows how much I believe them to be inferior, not only to the French, but also to the other civilized Nations of Europe."[60] Le Gentil's text exemplifies how attitudes toward China were changing in this period, as well as how previous views of Chinese technical, bureaucratic, and cultural achievements rankled an increasingly self-confident French nation determined to present itself, and Europe more generally, as preeminent. In bibliographic terms, his volume recalls texts like Le Comte's and anticipates Jean-Baptiste du Halde's better-known description of China from 1735. Some of the famous maps accompanying du Halde's tome, the product of collaboration among the Chinese emperor and his associates, European missionaries, and French geographers like Jean-Baptiste Bourguignon d'Anville, were acquired by Caylus, who donated at least one of them, representing the "Province de Quang-Si," to the French royal collections (Fig. 16).[61] Like Le Gentil's charts, it too is ornamented with arabesques and evokes dance diagrams. However, the hierarchies it proposes, such as the labeling of a blank area at the top of the map (next to the same province where Watteau's "Chinese woman" originated, Fig. 13) as inhabited by "*peuples sauvages*," relates as much if not more to Qing power dynamics as to European perspectives.

In 1727 Morville and his father were dismissed from government, and he and his wife began spending more time at their newly acquired country estate in the company of their troupe. Morville also expanded his art collection, including paintings that inspired some of the group's performances—notably Coypel's *City Love* and *Country Love* from 1731, both of which were engraved the following year (see Fig. 25, which notes the presence of an enslaved attendant in *City Love*).[62] Coypel's paintings likely inspired the play by Caylus for which the *Ballet des Porcelaines* served as a divertissement, entitled *The Ages, or the Fairy du Loreau*. The plot centers on a fairy who alters the ages of three types of couples—city lovers, country lovers, and older lovers—so

FIGURE 16

Jean-Baptiste Bourguignon d'Anville and collaborators, "Province de Quang-Si," from Jean-Baptiste du Halde, *Description . . . de l'Empire de la Chine* (Paris: P. G. le Mercier, 1735). Etching and engraving, 27 × 41 cm. Bibliothèque nationale de France, Paris. © Gallica BnF.

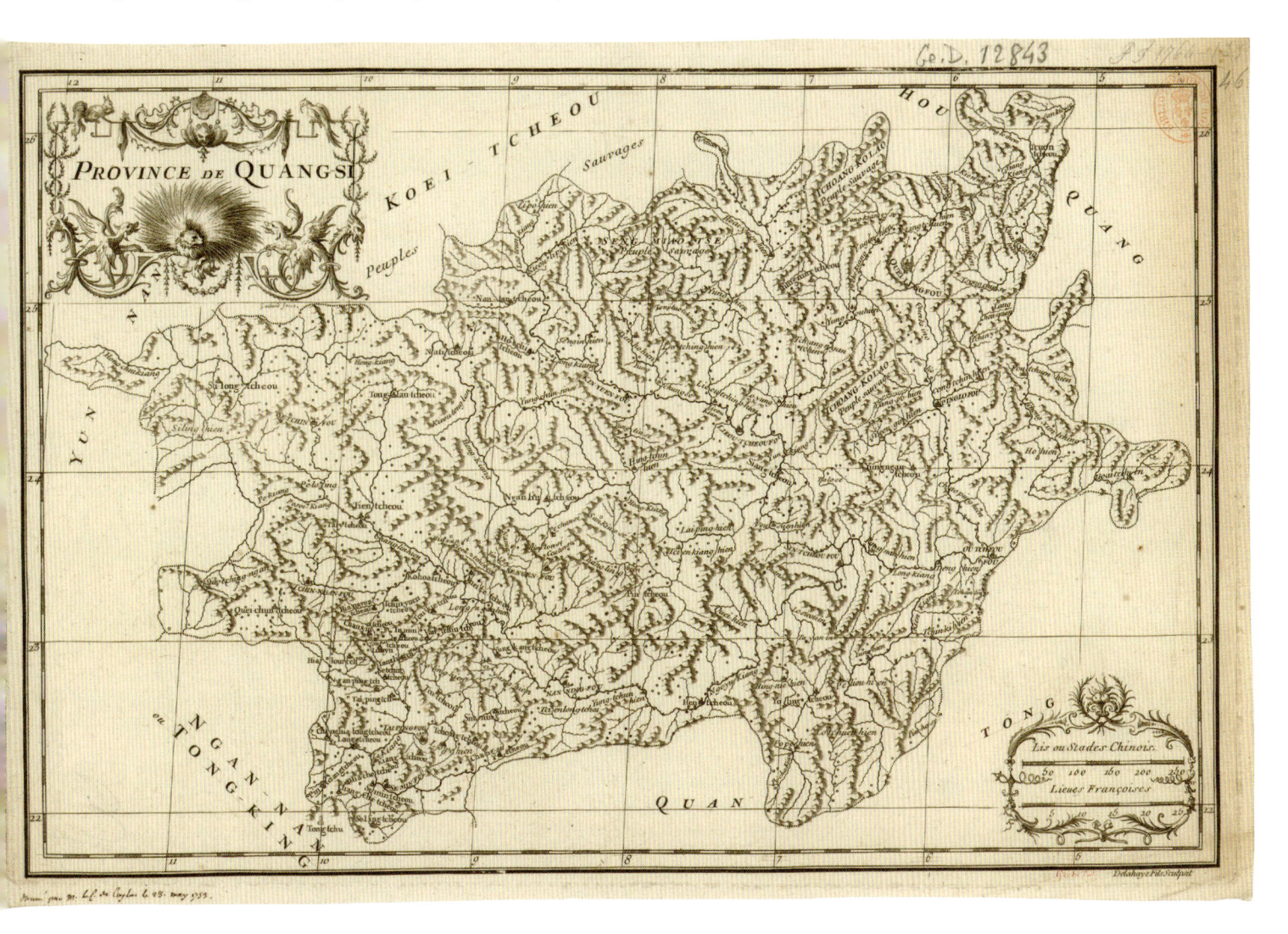

as to test the sincerity of their affections; Caylus himself performed the role of the peasant narrator, Mathurin.[63]

In 1739 *The Ages* was followed by the ballet, which was surely inspired by the comte de Morville's extensive porcelain collection. Some of this collection had been owned by his parents, although he sold off a good bit of it in 1729, a year after his father died.[64] He and his wife continued to buy more porcelain, possibly with the help of Gersaint, who claimed in his memoirs that Madame de Morville helped him obtain access to art collections in Holland.[65] From the mid-1730s Gersaint began advertising his services as a dealer specializing in Chinese goods and other "curiosities," and in 1739, the same year the *Ballet des Porcelaines* debuted, he changed the name of his shop to "*À la Pagode*"

in homage to the figures that epitomized Sino-French commerce.[66] To announce this
shift in his business model, Gersaint commissioned a new trade card designed by
Boucher and engraved by Caylus, portraying a stage-like interior littered with Asian
"props" (including a porcelain tea set) that genuflect and pay tribute to the giant
pagod looming overhead (Fig. 17). The card's design may even cannily cite *Perinet* or the
ballet in the form of this grotesque figure who, like his alter ego the Teapot Prince,
perches atop the lacquer cabinet and appears ready to hurl himself off it.

Morville's posthumous inventory reveals how he maintained, expanded, and modified his family's porcelain collection, keeping several of the Asian pieces—among them Chinese and Japanese plates and vases—while adding bronze-mounted celadon bowls and polychrome vases likely decorated in the *famille verte* and Kakiemon styles. He also collected European porcelain identified in his inventory as Saint-Cloud or Meissen, including a Meissen white teapot, and he owned a pair of pagods outfitted as small candelabra that may have resembled a pair now at The Metropolitan Museum of Art (Fig. 18).[67] Overall his taste was in keeping with that of his social and professional circles, which were deeply intertwined. As Marc Fumaroli has noted, cultural practices of collecting, socializing, and performing were essentially "aspects of government policy," enabling elite participants to forge or maintain important sociopolitical networks and show that they weren't just cogs in a state machine but deeply cultivated men.[68] Morville may have begun developing his own network years earlier through his attendance at Parisian gatherings hosted by Antoine Crozat, a powerful financier and art collector who, from 1712 to 1717, owned the exclusive right to conduct trade (including human trafficking) in French colonial Louisiana. Caylus and Coypel were also members of this circle, and they became close to Morville, composing and etching his epitaph after his death in 1732.[69] They continued to maintain strong ties to Morville's widow, Charlotte-Elisabeth de Vienne (1687–1761), who kept the group together over the next decade, including the period coinciding with the *Ballet des Porcelaines*.[70]

As noted earlier, nearly all of the Morville troupe members had high-level government connections: Amelot de Chaillou took over Morville's post as foreign secretary from 1737–44, and his daughter Anne (who probably danced the role of the princess) was married to Morville's son, the marquis d'Armenonville, a talented actor and army officer who was killed in 1742 during the War of the Austrian Succession. Amelot was a patron of Jean-Baptiste de Sade, another member of the group (as well as the father of the notorious marquis de Sade), who was appointed ambassador to the elector of Cologne in 1741.[71] Amelot's former brother-in-law, Pierre-Paul Bombarde de Beaulieu, had professional theater connections: in 1741, he became superintendent of the Paris Opéra. Lastly, one of Morville's daughters was married to Alexandre-Nicolas de La Rochefoucauld, marquis de Surgères, another army officer, amateur actor, and collector whose library inventory suggests the group's literary proclivities. In addition to Ovid's *Metamorphoses*, the list includes chivalric and pastoral romances, Orientalist fairy tales, travel accounts of East Asia and other foreign lands, and texts by Voltaire and Claude Prosper Jolyot de Crébillon (known as Crébillon fils), who were both friends of the group.[72] The latter's *Le Sopha* of 1742 (which Surgères owned) could, in fact, have been loosely inspired by *Perinet* or the ballet: it too tells the story of a young male courtier from "the Indies" who is transformed into an exotic object—in this case, a sofa—and forced to narrate the sexual exploits of his sitters until he is saved by love and restored to human form.

A key member of the Morville coterie, the comte de Caylus shared the group's pedigree, background, and interests. Born at Versailles, his mother had been a cousin and a favorite of Louis XIV's wife, Madame de Maintenon. Both he and his brother were supported by Jean-Frédéric Phélypeaux, comte de Maurepas, a powerful statesman and theater lover who, from 1723 to 1749, served as France's naval minister and director of colonial and maritime trade. (Maurepas took over the

FIGURE 18

Candelabrum with a pagod, c. 1740–48 (porcelain figure); c. 1740–50 (mounts). Villeroy manufactory, soft-paste porcelain with gilt-bronze mounts, 15.9 × 18.4 × 12.4 cm. The Metropolitan Museum of Art, Gift of Mr. and Mrs. Charles Wrightsman, 1976 (1976.155.27).

position from Morville; both of their fathers had held it before them.) Caylus fashioned himself as an author, engraver, antiquarian, and *amateur*, a new kind of influential figure in the Parisian art world who was affiliated with various academies and advised on matters of taste and collecting.[73] In more intimate circles, however, he loved to poke fun at serious academic pursuits, write libertine verse, and act in comic productions, often playing the role of the Savoyard or the peasant, as he did in *The Ages*.[74] He was a devoted collector of Asian goods, including porcelain, a costly fad mocked both in the 1741 prologue to the ballet and in a contemporaneous play by Coypel entitled *Curioso-manie*.[75] Like the practice of masquerade, these tongue-in-cheek performances served to bind groups like the Morville society more closely to each other and to affirm, through temporary satire or subversion, their sense of superiority and privilege. One can glean a sense of the bacchanalian atmosphere the group cultivated at Morville from a 1735 painting by the artist Nicolas Lancret, who was loosely connected to the group, entitled *Ham Luncheon* (Fig. 19). Though commissioned for Louis XV's *petits appartements* at Versailles, its vision of a close circle of white European elites (and one African attendant in a turban) partying in a garden, chilling wine in Saint-Cloud white porcelain coolers, and decadently smashing Kakiemon or Kakiemon-inspired plates captures the kind of pre- or post-performance revelries the society might have enjoyed.[76]

Although Caylus's younger brother was a distant member of the circle, his activities during the 1730s and '40s, as recounted in letters he received from Maurepas and the Morville clan, reveal interconnections between artistic creations like the *Ballet des Porcelaines* and French politics, commerce, and colonialism. During this period, Charles de Tubières de Pastel de Levoy de Grimoire, marquis de Caylus (1698–1750; I will call him "Charles" to distinguish him from his older brother) was a naval officer based at the Mediterranean port of Toulon, although he had loftier ambitions and repeatedly entreated Maurepas to send him on missions abroad. His main job seems to have been protecting French ships from Ottoman and North African corsairs, but in 1731 he was also tasked with mapping and surveying Tabarka, an island off the coast of Tunisia that Louis XV wanted to "acquire" to reap profits from coral fishing.[77] In 1734, Charles asked to be sent to America to "hunt interlopers" (presumably meaning privateers, but perhaps also European rivals and native inhabitants), but war prevented him from going until the end of the decade. Stuck at port, he complained of being inactive, while sending small gifts to his supporters (tobacco, a roll of *toile peinte*, a parrot to his brother) to advance his cause.[78] His friends responded in letters that sought to alleviate his boredom by recounting stage performances and other happenings in and around Paris, including news of the Morville troupe. In 1740, Maurepas's secretary, Alexandre Sallé (illegitimate son of the actress Charlotte Desmares) wrote to inform Charles of the marriage of one of Morville's daughters—which was, incidentally, the reason given in the 1741 prologue for the two-year delay between performances of the *Ballet des Porcelaines*.[79]

Eventually Charles's persistence paid off, and in 1745 he was named governor of France's Windward Islands (*Îles du Vent*), which included the West Indian colonies of Martinique and Guadeloupe. His appointment may have reflected the Caylus family's history in the region, including their presumed relation to Jean-Baptiste de Caylus, a French engineer who, using enslaved labor, built the fortress of Martinique's colonial capital and may have also authored a treatise on chocolate and

sugar.[80] Most accounts of Charles's five-year tenure as governor focus on his inept-itude and corruption, but a report submitted in 1749 attempts to paint his actions in a more positive light. Written for Antoine Louis Rouillé, Maurepas's successor, it details the myriad ways Charles had attempted to bring "order" and "discipline" to the islands, so as to make commerce and agriculture "flourish," expand France's colonial presence in the region, and bring the colonies "to a state of perfection" that would enhance the monarchy's global standing.[81] Much of the report concerns the islands' enslaved populations, which numbered nearly sixty thousand in Mar-tinique in 1736, as compared with roughly fifteen thousand whites.[82] In addition to reestablishing royal authority over the procurement and treatment of enslaved men and women, Charles endeavored to increase their numbers, particularly for sugar production—a colonial commodity intrinsically linked to porcelain that, by the 1740s, had become indispensable among the European elite. He also sought to recapture enslaved runaways, create an island militia, expand the transatlantic trade, and enact a plan hatched by his counterpart in New France to enslave Indig-enous "sauvages" from that colony and transport them to the *Îles du Vent*.[83]

Although little of Charles's story made its way into the ballet (which was writ-ten years before he became governor), it offers a telling bookend to the comte de Morville's activities, indicating how members of this group served as driving forces of French commerce and colonialism from the 1720s to '40s—a period that also corresponded with the rise and proliferation of *chinoiserie*. In an important study, Madeleine Dobie has explored how the West and East Indies (or the New World and the "Orient") were linked in eighteenth-century France, arguing for "a kind of 'continental drift' whereby French economic interests in the Atlantic colonies were transposed into a fashion for things oriental."[84] Dobie further argues that owing to its "disturbing" nature, colonial slavery was mostly absent from French literary and cultural representations until about the 1760s, or rather it was "projected onto other geopolitical contexts," namely the Oriental sphere, along with depictions of Oriental despotism and *chinoiserie*.[85] Dobie's argument focuses on French liter-ature and philosophy rather than the visual, material, or performing arts, where, I would argue, colonial slavery was not so invisible—as evidenced, for example, by the extremely popular Gobelins tapestry series known as the *Anciennes Indes* and *Nouvelles Indes*, which depict enslaved Africans laboring to produce sugar in a co-lonial landscape. (Studies for the *Nouvelles Indes* were shown at the Paris Salons of 1737, 1738, 1740, and 1741.)[86] Moreover, it seems clear that members of the Morville circle did not find New World slavery disturbing: in fact, among the "gifts" Charles gave to his brother was an enslaved man from Martinique, whom Caylus kept in his household for fifteen years before freeing him in 1763.[87] Identified in Caylus's personal papers as "son mulâtre, de Martinique," the man's name is listed as Guil-laume Chably. It isn't clear how he got it, but "Guillaume" is also the name of the protagonist in Caylus's *Histoire de Guillaume Cocher* (c. 1730), a libertine tale starring a Parisian coachman who narrates the exploits of his elite European clientele.

Slavery is not explicitly referenced in the *Ballet des Porcelaines*, whose "hidden" meaning seems to relate more to the desire to appropriate the secrets of porcelain manufacture as well as to control the influx of Asian goods into France, a feat the French had never really been able to master. Even so, it is essential to note the extent to which slavery, international commerce, and proto-industrial production were linked through global capitalism—a massive, far-reaching phenomenon that could be embodied by something as tiny and seemingly innocuous as a porcelain cup filled with chocolate or tea. The ballet and its literary source did not have to expressly invoke colonial slavery or the New World for audiences to conjure these and other associations: eighteenth-century authors and artists often conflated the East and West Indies, sometimes for strategic purposes, whereas the pervasive trope of "enchanted islands" could bring to mind any number of exotic and colonial locales.[88] The ballet's theme of captivity and subsequent liberation from a despotic foreign power, who has the magical ability to turn men into *meubles* (moveable property, the term used to define enslaved humans in France's 1685 *Code Noir*), could have resonated in many different ways, while ending on a triumphalist note for the prince and princess and, by extension, for the French elites who incarnated and likely identified with them.[89]

The theme of a victorious France conquering, civilizing, or Christianizing the globe was a common one in ballets around this time (including *Les Indes galantes*), and it drew on older imagery of the Four Continents that divided the world into racialized geographical categories, with Europe usually viewed as ascendant. Prior to this period, court entertainments known as "Ballets des Nations" likewise tended to place France and its nobility at the top of the global hierarchy, and to depict other countries and cultures through gestures and costumes that gradually became conventionalized and racialized.[90] But one could go further and say that even without an explicit message of European preeminence, the entire "corporeal episteme" of classical ballet (and, in particular, the *danse noble*) as it was conceived and practiced at Louis XIV's court and beyond can be interpreted as embodying a feeling of superiority over others—one that could have trickled down to less overtly bombastic, "diverting" dances like the *Ballet des Porcelaines*. Noting that the *danse noble* emerged amid an era of intense political, commercial, and colonial expansion in France, Susan Leigh Foster has asked whether this broad context might have encouraged French and European protagonists to experience and express their own bodies as powerful and dominant.[91]

Not only did court ballet have deep military roots, but it presupposed an internally disciplined, integrated "center" (often associated with the king) that moved forward and extended outward, appropriating and occupying space in its path.[92] That process is visualized in the Beauchamp-Feuillet system of dance notation that Louis XIV commissioned in the 1670s—at the height of his own expansionist ambitions—as a way to maintain a record of court dances that could then be reproduced and circulated. Several notations were published in 1700, including some for Jean-Baptiste Lully's opera *Bellérophon*, which celebrated France's military victories over the Netherlands. One of them depicts the feet of four dancers (labeled "B, A, A, B" at the bottom of the page) who proceed downstage together along an implied central axis with "immanent force" (as Sarah

FIGURE 20

Raoul-Auger Feuillet, "Balet de neuf danseurs," from *Recueil de dances, composée par M. Feuillet . . .* (Paris: l'auteur, 1700), 68. Etching, 24 × 17.5 cm. Bibliothèque nationale de France, Paris. © Gallica BnF.

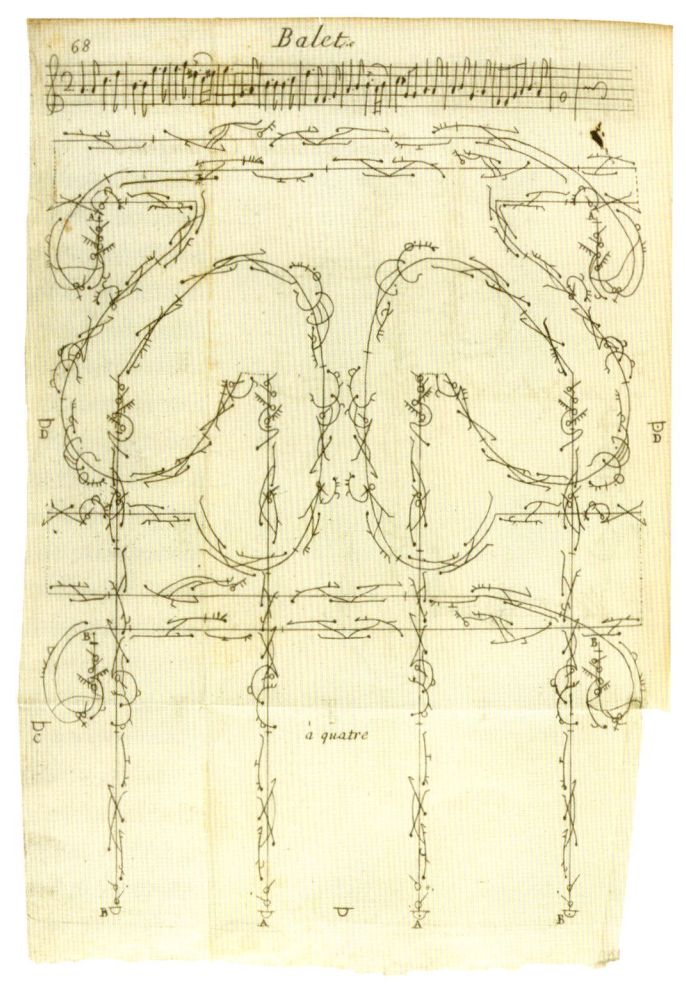

porcelain and human bodies—both originally made (according to the Bible) out of clay, both covered with "skin," both fashioned into curvaceous shapes—this print, made by the Augsburg engraver Martin Engelbrecht around 1730, also hints at how the bodies of laborers were subsumed into the objects they produced, even as their labor was being made invisible through global capitalism or the magic of commodity fetishism. For their part, the Morville coterie probably got an extra kick out of watching servants traverse the stage in porcelain costumes, whereas the servants may have viewed it as an extension of the domestic drudgery (including the carrying, serving, and cleaning of porcelain) they performed every day.

FIGURE 21

Martin Engelbrecht, "Porcelain maker," 1700–56. Hand-colored etching and engraving, 35.7 x 22 cm. Winterthur Museum, Gift of Henry Francis du Pont (1955.0135.008). Courtesy of Winterthur Museum.

FIGURE 22

Piero Bonifazio Algieri, Detail of a maquette for the stage design of Act III of Jean-Philippe Rameau's *Les Paladins*, 1760. Gouache, gold, and silver on cardboard, 42.5 × 53.5 cm. Château de Champs-sur-Marne. © Reproduction Benjamin Gavaudo / CMN.

Both the sorcerer and the servants likely enacted some of the stereotypical poses and steps identified with China in eighteenth-century Europe, including acrobatic leaps and raised index fingers (see Fig. 26).[102] Although these gestures have a still-debated origin, they contributed to increasingly racialized stereotypes of Chinese peoples that persist in ballet productions to this day—as shown by Phil Chan's essay in this volume, along with his activist work through the organization Final Bow for Yellowface.[103] China may have been described in some early modern European travel accounts as a supremely civilized empire that was equal or superior to France, but in the world of eighteenth-century French ballet, Chinese dancers were nearly always represented in a comic or grotesque mode that underscored their difference relative to European elites, and sometimes also the corrosive pleasures they signaled.

In a review of the 1754 pantomime ballet *Les Jardins Chinois*, which premiered in Paris at almost exactly the same time as Noverre's *Les Fêtes Chinoises*, the French critic Pierre de Morand condemned the "*magot* attitudes" of the dancers, their "contortions, grimaces, miens [that were] so disgraceful to see." Morand worried that these "forced, unnatural steps" would "destroy" any "good taste" that the European art of dancing had left, just as other Chinese "frivolities" had "destroyed [the taste] we had for other arts."[104] As for Noverre's ballet, Morand chastised the chinamania it had generated, noting that he expected "inevitably to see palanquins on the streets of Paris," and that "it would also be very nice to see men with tailed mustaches (*moustaches à queue*) and drooping goatees there."[105] Sometimes these grotesque dancers were pitted against Asian theatrical characters, like the protagonists of Voltaire's *L'Orphelin de la Chine* (1753), who conformed to a moralizing, patriarchal ideal that was presented as Chinese but that mirrored contemporary Enlightenment, Western constructs. One year after Voltaire's play (based on a thirteenth-century Chinese work) premiered in Paris in 1755, it was followed by a burlesque parody entitled *Les Magots*.[106] *Magots* or pagods also appeared on stage in Act III of Rameau's opera *Les Paladins* (1760), where a group of dancers dressed as porcelain pagods began bobbing their heads, coming to life, and dancing around in a comically grotesque way.[107] A detail from Piero Bonifazio Algieri's over-the-top surviving stage design, which depicts two-dimensional cardboard pagods ornamenting a sumptuous palace, suggests what the costumes and poses of the dancers performing on stage would have looked like (Fig. 22). Their stereotypical movements, props, and features—conical hats, umbrellas, drooping mustaches, rounded bellies—would have been drawn both from earlier court masquerades and from "nodding" porcelain prototypes (see Figs. 4 and 7).

In *Perinet*, the prince and princess triumph at the end while the sorcerer is reduced to a pagod; in Caylus's ballet, he simply "runs away and disappears," and the ballet ends with a *contredanse*. Introduced at the French court during the 1680s, the *contredanse* was a "Frenchified" version of the English country dance, and it was arguably more "sociable" and less hierarchical than the *danse noble*, particularly when performed by members of different classes.[108] In a *contredanse*, the bodies of couples moved in unison and created elegant patterns and circles like those seen in André Lorin's *Livre de la contredanse du Roy*, devised for Louis XIV in the 1680s (Fig. 23). We can assume that the ballet's finale looked something like the dances in Lorin's book, and that its serpentine patterns would have recalled the circles that the prince and the sorcerer had danced around each other, even if the *contredanse* was meant to embody harmony rather than discord or menace. And yet *contredanses*, despite their appearance of inclusion, could be closed circles: intended, like *théâtres de société*, to bind like-minded elites more firmly to each other, or, like masquerade, to present a brief disruption or subversion of hierarchical categories before returning to and reinforcing the status quo.[109] Whereas those with money or connections might succeed in buying into this circle, their inclusion often occurred at the expense of others who had to be cast out of it.

Coda: Curtain Call

Like the vessels it triumphantly shatters, the *Ballet des Porcelaines* exists only in fragments, which makes reimagining it both an exciting opportunity and a daunting challenge. Phil Chan and I, together with our creative team, have spent countless hours researching and discussing the project, and early on we made the decision to tell the ballet's story from a different point of view, namely by giving movement, voice, agency, and nuance to Asian characters too often presented in European ballet as ridiculous or ornamental. Phil's essay explains the thinking and the process behind this vision and the ways it shaped his choreography and casting choices, Harriet Jung's costumes, and Sugar Vendil's "kintsugi" music. *Kintsugi*—a Japanese technique for repairing broken ceramics by mending them with gold or lacquer so as to highlight their imperfections—serves in fact as a metaphor for the entire project, which acknowledges the potentially denigrating stereotypes inherent in ballet, *chinoiserie*, and other cultural forms while also seeing the potential to salvage their fragile beauty and make them resonate with our present moment. In a recent

FIGURE 23

André Lorin, "Contredance du Roy," from *Livre de contredance du roy, présenté à Louis XIV* (1688), *et retranscrit pour Louis XIV* (1721). Bibliothèque nationale de France, Département des Manuscrits, Paris.
© Gallica BnF.

lecture on "ornamentalism," her influential theory of Asiatic femininity, Anne Anlin Cheng asked "what beauty might look like in a broken world," illustrating a work by the Korean artist Yeesookyung, who creates new sculptures out of ceramic shards smashed in earlier periods, as a possible response (Fig. 24; see also Fig. 30).[110] In my view, Phil's choreography asks and answers this question as well.

Writing this essay, I am keenly aware that though the historical record may be fragmented, the elite members of the Morville troupe (and its male members in particular) left behind copious traces in the form of archival documents, inventories, letters, portraits, art collections, and publications. This is not true, of course, for the Morville servants who performed as porcelain vessels, and who were obliged to fill in to some extent for absent or imagined Chinese bodies, given that very few visitors came to France from China during the eighteenth century and none, to my knowledge, performed on stage. Like the many thousands of laborers involved in making porcelain and other goods for eighteenth-century global consumption, the identities of the servants obliged to take part in such performances are mostly unknown, and their responses to such productions are mostly unrecorded. There is, however, at least one revealing instance of "pushback": in January 1763, following a production of Jean-Jacques Rousseau's pastoral opera *Le devin du village* (The Village Soothsayer) at the Parisian home of the French nobleman Christophe-Louis Pajot de Villers, a coachman in Villers' employ named Nicolas Dandeli got up on stage, dropped his trousers, and, while the curtain was lowered, mooned the audience of aristocrats who were starting to exit the room. An adolescent Black attendant named Capolin, who was most likely enslaved, raised the curtain, making the coachman's bare bum visible to the guests. As Jeff Ravel has noted, the event may have been prompted by rivalry between the two servants, but it can also be interpreted as an act of resistance from below—one that sought to expose the hypocrisy of an elite society who might have embraced egalitarian ideals presented onstage or on the page, but who continued to subjugate those whom they perceived as inferior in life.[111]

FIGURE 24

Yeesookyung, *Translated Vase*, 2007. Ceramic fragments, epoxy, and gold leaf, 66.7 × 51.4 × 42.5 cm. The David and Alfred Smart Museum of Art, The University of Chicago; Purchase, Gift of Gay-Young Cho and Christopher Chiu in honor of Richard A. Born.

Invento et peint par Ch. Coypel 1781.　　　　　　　*Gravé par Lepicié 1782.*

L'AMOUR DE VILLE, OU L'AMOUR COQUET

Loin de l'innocence des bois,
Pour le fidelle amour il n'est point de retraitte;
A la ville on suit d'autres loix,
Et c'est un jeu pour la coquette
De tromper deux cœurs à la fois.

a Paris, chez L.Surugue graveur du Roy rüe des Noyers vis avis St Yves　　　*A.P.D.R.*

Capolin appears to have been owned by the sister of Alexandre Rouillé de Raucourt, Charles de Caylus's successor as colonial governor of Martinique, who "gave" him to the Villers family for "safekeeping."[112] The year of the mooning incident, 1763, was also the year the comte de Caylus freed Guillaume Chably after fifteen years of enslavement in France. Given the timing, Chably does not seem to have been in France when the *Ballet des Porcelaines* was performed, but it is possible that other enslaved individuals who served the Morville coterie, and whose names and identities are lost to us today, were there. Despite the common assumption that "there were no slaves" in early modern France (i.e., that slavery could exist only in the colonies, not the

[26] Robert Hornback, *Racism and Early Blackface Comic Traditions: From the Old World to the New* (Cham, Switzerland: Palgrave Macmillan, 2018), chap. 2. In a letter recounting the fête, the Swedish architect Daniel Cronström connected the duc's costume to Harlequin; see https://catalogue.bnf.fr/ark:/12148/cb42403784z. In 1723, *Arlequin barbet, pagode et médecin* by Alain-René Lesage and Jacques-Philippe d'Orneval, in which Harlequin impersonated a pagod, was performed at the Foire Saint-Germain.

[27] The grotesque or arabesque in both dance and art has been interpreted along these lines in Sarah Cohen, *Art, Dance, and the Body in French Culture of the Ancien Régime* (Cambridge: Cambridge University Press, 2000), chap. 3. See also Katie Scott, *The Rococo Interior: Decoration and Social Spaces in Early Eighteenth-Century Paris* (New Haven and London: Yale University Press, 1995).

[28] On this development, which is exemplified by the "it-narrative" and other eighteenth-century cultural forms, see Julie Park, *The Self and It: Novel Objects in Eighteenth-Century England* (Stanford: Stanford University Press, 2010).

[29] Louis Le Comte, *Memoirs and Observations*, quoted in David Pullins, "L'introuvable peinture chinoise de François Boucher ou la question de la caricature," in *Une des provinces du rococo: La Chine rêvée de François Boucher*, ed. Yohan Rimaud, exh. cat. (Besançon: Musée des beaux-arts et d'archéologie, 2019): "il serait à souhaiter que les desseins dont les Chinois se servent dans la peinture et la porcelaine fussent plus beaux [. . .] les figures humains y sont toutes estropiées."

[30] Gerritsen and McDowall, "Material Culture and the Other," 103.

[31] Perrin Stein, "Les chinoiseries de Boucher et leurs sources: l'art de l'appropriation," in *Pagodes et Dragons. Exotisme et fantaisie dans l'Europe rococo 1720–1770*, ed. Georges Brunel, exh. cat. (Paris: Musée Cernuschi, 2007): 92–94.

[32] Robert Finlay, "The Pilgrim Art: The Culture of Porcelain in World History," *Journal of World History* 9, 2 (Fall 1988): 175.

[33] In the *Encyclopédie* (1751–65), Diderot described pagods (or *magots*, an alternate name for these figures, discussed below) as "coliflichets prétieux dont la nation s'est entêtée," quoted in Kisluk-Grosheide, "The Reign of Magots and Pagods," 184. See also Huguette Cohen, "Diderot and the Image of China in Eighteenth-Century France," *Studies on Voltaire and the Eighteenth Century* 242 (1986): 219–32.

[34] Anne Perrin Khelissa, "Menace sur le 'grand' art. Le peuple des magots et des statuettes en porcelaine au Siècle des Lumières," in *Penser le 'petit' de l'Antiquité au premier xxᵉ siècle: Approches textuelles et pratiques de la miniaturisation artistique* (Lyon: Fage, 2017): 88–98. On Caylus's collection, see Cordélia Hattori, "Le comte de Caylus d'après les archives," *Les Cahiers d'histoire de l'art* 5 (2007): 54–70. On the derogatory associations of these figures, see David Pullins, "L'introuvable peinture chinoise," and Christopher Johns, *China and the Church: Chinoiserie in Global Context* (Oakland: University of California Press, 2016), 121–24. Johns argues that these figures took on "decidedly negative connotations" by the 1730s, but I would argue that these associations emerged earlier and coexisted with what Johns describes as a more positive view of Chinese bodies (particularly royal or imperial bodies) during the late seventeenth century.

[35] Volk, "Dehua Porcelain Figures of Budai," 22, fig. 17.

[36] See The Metropolitan Museum of Art's online entry, https://www.metmuseum.org/art/collection/search/207247?searchField=All&sortBy=Relevance&ft=shou+lao+chantilly&offset=0&rpp=20&pos=1. Chi-ming Yang makes a similar claim about how decorative art objects, and specifically French porcelain, "shaped the emergence of new racial thinking in the eighteenth century" in "Elephantine Chinoiserie and Asian Whiteness: Views on a Pair of Sèvres Vases," *The Journal of the Walters Art Museum* 75 (2021), https://journal.thewalters.org/2021/05/elephantine-chinoiserie-and-asian-whiteness-views-on-a-pair-of-sevres-vases/. On Bernier's essay, "A New Division of the Earth by Different Species or Races of Men," and its description of East Asian peoples, see Michael Keevak, *Becoming Yellow: A Short History of Racial Thinking* (Princeton: Princeton University Press, 2011), 46–50; and Pierre H. Boulle, "François Bernier and the Origins of the Modern Conception of Race," in *The Color of Liberty: Histories of Race in France*, ed. Sue Peabody and Tyler Edward Stovall (Durham: Duke University Press, 2003), 11–27.

[37] Pullins, "L'introuvable peinture chinoise," 128.

[38] Nicole Garnier-Pelle and Monelle Hayot, *Les singeries du château de Chantilly = The Monkey Rooms* (Paris: Nicolas Chaudun, 2013).

[39] The connection between eighteenth-century singeries and nineteenth-century racist theories linking monkeys and men was made in the 2021 Musée d'Orsay exhibition *Les origines du monde: l'invention de la nature au xixᵉ siècle*. See also Johns, *China and the Church*, 124–27; and Diane Fourny, "A Strange Familiarity: Monkeys and Chinamen in Enlightenment France," *The French Review* 92, 4 (May 2019): 157–74.

[40] Madame de Villeneuve's companion, the playwright Prosper Jolyot de Crébillon, was attached to the house of Bourbon-Condé, and his son Crébillon fils was a member of the Morville troupe. The wife of another troupe member, Jean-Baptiste de Sade (father of the marquis de Sade; see below), was lady-in-waiting to the princesse de Condé. See also Virginia E. Swain, "Beauty's Chambers: Mixed Styles and Mixed Messages in Villeneuve's *Beauty and the Beast*," *Marvels & Tales* 19, 2 (2005): 197–223.

[41] Kimberly J. Lau, "Imperial Marvels: Race and the Colonial Imagination in the Fairy Tales of Madame d'Aulnoy," *Narrative Culture* 3, 2 (Fall 2016): 141–79. Lau (160, 173) notes that d'Aulnoy seems to have been familiar with the writings of François Bernier, both his work on human-animal boundaries and his essay on racial classification.

[42] See the introduction to Gabrielle-Suzanne Barbot de Villeneuve, *Beauty and the Beast: The Original Story*, ed. and trans. Aurora Wolfgang (Toronto: Iter Press, 2020), 58–68; and Kylie Sago, "Colonial Encounters of 'La Belle et la Bête'," in *Encounters in the Arts, Literature, and Philosophy: Chance and Choice*, ed. Jérôme Brillaud and Virginie Greene (London: Bloomsbury Academic, 2021): 59–69.

43 An anthology published in 1786 attributes it to the chevalier de Mailly, although the attribution is far from certain; see *Le prince Perinet ou l'origine des Pagodes*, in *Le cabinet des fées, ou collection choisie des contes de fées, et autres contes merveilleux* (Amsterdam and Paris, Rue et Hôtel Serpente, 1786), 31: 205–32. An elusive figure and author of many fairy tales, the chevalier de Mailly may have been the brother of Louis de Mailly, whose son-in-law, Louis Phélypeaux, marquis de La Vrillière, served as head of the navy ministry and secured a naval post for the comte de Caylus's brother (see below). Louis de Mailly's granddaughters became mistresses to Louis XV, and one of them, Marie Anne de Mailly-Nesle, duchesse de Châteauroux, commissioned one of the most celebrated French chinoiserie interiors of the eighteenth century, the so-called chambre bleue.

44 *Le prince Perinet ou l'origine des Pagodes*, 122: "un genie de la plus grosse espece."

45 Bertrand Rondot, ed., *Discovering the Secrets of Soft-Paste Porcelain at The Saint-Cloud Manufactory, ca.1690–1766* (New Haven and London: Published for The Bard Graduate Center for the Studies in the Decorative Arts by Yale University Press, 1999), 275, 279.

46 Keevak, *Becoming Yellow*. On the association of yellow with the emperor, see, for example, Le Gentil de La Barbinais, *Nouveau Voyage Autour du Monde* (Paris: Briasson, 1728), 2: 22.

47 *Le prince Perinet ou l'origine des Pagodes*, 125: "toutes les porcelaines en devinrent folles, et ne pouvoient être un moment sans joüer avec lui, & sans lui dire toutes les sottises que les femmes ne disent que trop à ses pareils." I am grateful to Jeffrey Collins for pointing this out and for helping me improve this essay in so many ways.

48 Stacey Sloboda, "Fashioning Bluestocking Conversation: Elizabeth Montagu's Chinese Room," in *Architectural Space in Eighteenth-Century Europe: Constructing Identities and Interiors*, ed. Denise Baxter and Meredith Martin (Farnham, UK: Ashgate, 2010), 138.

49 Anne Defrance, "La refraction des sciences dans le conte de fées," *Féeries* 6 (2009): 63–86.

50 Jones, *Shapely Bodies*, 186.

51 Charlotte Guichard, *Colonial Watteau: Commerce, Galanterie and Colonial Imagination in Regency France* (Berlin and Munich: Deutscher Kunstverlag, 2022). See also Alain Viala, *La France galante: Essai historique sur une catégorie culturelle, de ses origines jusqu'à la Révolution* (Paris: Presses Universitaires de France, 2008).

52 Scott, "Playing Games with Otherness," 196; "Inventaire après décès de Jeanne Gilbert, madame d'Armenonville (1716)," Archives nationales de France (hereafter AN), 6AP/12, fol.51v, n.172: "pagottes tenant chacune un enfant aussi de la Chine de deux pieds de haule."

53 Germain Boffrand, *Livre d'architecture* (Paris: Guillaume Cavelier, 1745), translated as *Book of Architecture: Containing the General Principles of the Art*, ed. Caroline van Eyck, trans. David Britt (Aldershot: Ashgate, 2002), 16.

54 The statue was still owned by the family at the time of Morville's death; see "Inventaire après décès de Charles Jean-Baptiste Fleriau, comte de Morville (1732)," AN, 6AP/10, fol.115r.

55 Scott, "Playing Games with Otherness," 227.

56 Stéphane Castelluccio, *Collecting Chinese and Japanese Porcelain in Pre-Revolutionary Paris* (Los Angeles: J. Paul Getty Museum, 2013), 27.

57 Rochelle Ziskin, *Sheltering Art: Collecting and Social Identity in Early Eighteenth-Century Paris* (University Park, PA: Pennsylvania State University Press, 2012), 168.

58 Morville's ministerial duties and contacts with ambassadors and merchants are detailed in "Estat des ordonnances de M. de Morville," Archives diplomatiques de La Courneuve, 53 MD/314.

59 "Mémoire envoyé au comte de Morville sur le commerce des Indes et de la mer du Sud," AN, MAR/B/7/118, fols. 119–22, 29 juillet 1724. On his involvement in Dutch East India Company trade regulations, see *Arrest du conseil d'éstat du roi, du 12 avril 1723, portant règlement pour l'entrée dans le royaume des étains de Siam, provenans de la Compagnie des Indes Orientales de Hollande* (Paris: Impr. de la veuve et M.-G. Jouvenel, 1723).

60 Le Gentil, *Nouveau Voyage*, "Épître à Monseigneur le comte de Morville," 2: 61, 69, 109: "J'estime les Chinois, mais cette estime ne m'aveugle pas jusqu'à leur attribuer la supériorité sur nous. Vous connoîtrez dans la suite combien je les crois inferieurs, non seulement aux François, mais encore aux autres Nations policées de l'Europe."

61 See the BnF's online entry for this map: https://catalogue.bnf.fr/ark:/12148/cb40741590x; and Mario Cams, "The China Maps of Jean-Baptiste Bourguignon d'Anville: Origins and Supporting Networks," *Imago Mundi: The International Journal for the History of Cartography* 66, 1 (2013): 51–69.

62 Esther Bell, "Charles-Antoine Coypel (1694–1752): Painting and Performance in Eighteenth-Century France" (PhD dissertation, Institute of Fine Arts, New York University, 2011), chap. 2. Bell argues compellingly for an "interdependence between private theatrical institutions and painting" in this period, particularly in connection with the Morville society. For more on Morville's collecting practices, see Ziskin, *Sheltering Art*.

63 Quéro, "De la 'société de Morville' au 'théâtre du château de Morville'," 42. See also n. 3.

64 AN, 6AP/10, "Procés verbal de vente des meubles après le décès de Monseigneur d'Armenonville."

65 Ziskin, *Sheltering Art*, 310.

66 Guillaume Glorieux, *À l'enseigne de Gersaint. Edmé-François Gersaint, marchand d'art sur le pont Notre-Dame (1694–1750)* (Seyssel: Champ vallon, 2002), 264–67.

67 AN, 6AP/10, "Inventaire [. . .] de comte de Morville," fols.150r-56r.

68 Marc Fumaroli, "Un gentilhomme universel: Anne-Claude de Thubières, comte de Caylus," in Joanot Martorell, *Tirant Le Blanc* (Paris: Gallimard, 1997), 612. See also the Introduction to *Histoire et recueil des Lazzis*, ed. Judith Curtis and David Alfred Trott (Oxford: Voltaire Foundation, 1996).

69 Caylus after Coypel, *Épitaphe du comte de Morville*, BnF, Département des Estampes et de la photographie, DB-7-FOL, p. 57. On the Crozat circle, see Ziskin, Sheltering Art.

70 Quéro, "De la 'société de Morville' au 'théâtre du château de Morville'." Unless otherwise noted, Quéro is also the source for the biographical information on the other troupe members recounted in the next paragraph.

71 Laurence L. Bongie, *Sade: A Biographical Essay* (Chicago and London: The University of Chicago Press, 1998), 21.

72 "Catalogue des livres du cabinet de monsieur le comte de Surgères (1761)," Bibliothèque interuniversitaire de la Sorbonne, MS 677.

73 Charlotte Guichard, "Taste Communities: The Rise of the 'Amateur' in Eighteenth-Century Paris," *Eighteenth Century Studies* 45, 4 (Summer 2012): 519–47.

74 Charlotte Guichard, "Connoisseurship: Art and Antiquities," and Perrin Stein, "Vases and Satire," in *The Saint-Aubin Livre de caricatures: Drawing Satire in Eighteenth-Century Paris*, ed. Colin Jones, Juliet Carey, and Emily Richardson (Oxford: Voltaire Foundation, 2012), chaps. 13 and 14.

75 Charles-Antoine Coypel, *La curiosimanie* (c.1740). See also "Feste donnée à Morville le 23 juin 1741"; and Esther Bell, "A Curator at the Louvre: Charles Coypel and the Royal Collections," *Journal18* Issue 2, *Louvre Local* (Fall 2016), https://www.journal18.org/986.

76 On this painting, see Mary Tavener Holmes and Joseph Focarino, *Nicolas Lancret: 1690–1743* (New York: Harry N. Abrams, 1991), 78. Holmes has written extensively about Lancret and has explored his intimate connection with the Paris theater and dance world, most notably in *Nicolas Lancret: Dance Before a Fountain* (Los Angeles: The J. Paul Getty Museum, 2006). In addition to Marie Sallé (whose Lancret portrait inspired a porcelain figure made by the Höchst manufactory in the 1750s; see Elizabeth Rouget's essay in this volume), the artist also depicted the actor son of Grandval, the ballet's composer.

77 The letters sent to Charles de Caylus by Maurepas and others were apparently seized by an English ship during their transfer from Toulon to Martinique, and are transcribed in *Report on the Manuscripts of Lady Du Cane* (London: Ben Johnson and Co., 1905). For Tabarka, see Maurepas to Caylus, May 23, 1731, 248–49.

78 *Report on the Manuscripts of Lady Du Cane*, letters dated October 20, 1734; December 8, 1734; December 18, 1740; and September 16, 1741.

79 *Report on the Manuscripts of Lady Du Cane*, Sallé to Caylus, letter dated December 18, 1740. See also "Feste donnée à Morville le 23 juin 1741."

80 Quélus (Jean-Baptiste de Caylus?), *Histoire naturelle du cacao et du sucre* (Paris: L. d'Houry, 1719); Benjamin Steiner, *Building the French Empire, 1600–1800: Colonialism and Material Culture* (Manchester: Manchester University Press, 2020), chap. 3.

81 "Sommaire des maximes et des vues du marquis de Caylus dans l'administration des Isles françoises du Vent de l'Amérique et des lettres qu'il a écrit en consequence (1749)," Archives nationales d'outre mer, COL C8 A 58, esp. fol. 296. On Charles's corruption, see, for example, James Pritchard, "The Naval Career of a Colonial Governor: Charles de Thubières, Marquis de Caylus, 1698–1750," *Proceedings of the Meeting of the French Colonial History Society* 16 (1992): 12–23.

82 K.G. Davies, *The North Atlantic World in the Seventeenth Century* (Minneapolis: University of Minnesota Press, 1974), 83; Franklin W. Knight, ed., *General History of the Caribbean, Volume III: The Slave Societies of the Caribbean* (New York: Palgrave Macmillan; Paris: UNESCO Publishing, 2007), 38. The slave trade was most active in the region between 1725 and 1760.

83 "Sommaire des maximes et des vues du marquis de Caylus," fols. 300, 301, 327.

84 Madeleine Dobie, "Orientalism, Colonialism, and Furniture in Eighteenth-Century France," in *Furnishing the Eighteenth Century: What Furniture Can Tell Us about the European and American Past*, ed. Dena Goodman and Kathryn Norberg (London: Routledge, 2007), 14. Dobie's argument aligns somewhat with Kimberly Lau's in "Imperial Marvels," in which Lau maintains that a deep engagement with the New World and issues of race, slavery, and colonialism were critical to the development of French fairy tales (specifically those of Madame d'Aulnoy), even if overt references are invisible.

85 Madeleine Dobie, *Trading Places: Colonization and Slavery in Eighteenth-Century French Culture* (Ithaca: Cornell University Press, 2010).

86 Charissa Bremer-David, "Le Cheval Rayé: A French Tapestry Portraying Dutch Brazil," *J. Paul Getty Museum Journal* 22 (1994): 23.

87 Hattori, "Le comte de Caylus d'après les archives," 57.

88 Mary Sheriff, *Enchanted Islands: Picturing the Allure of Conquest in Eighteenth-Century France* (Chicago: The University of Chicago Press, 2018); Ashley L. Cohen, *The Global Indies: British Imperial Culture and the Reshaping of the World, 1756–1815* (New Haven: Yale University Press, 2021).

89 Jennifer L. Palmer, *Intimate Bonds: Family and Slavery in the French Atlantic* (Philadelphia: University of Pennsylvania Press, 2016), 46, 50.

90 Ellen R. Welch, "Dancing the Nation: Performing France in the Seventeenth-Century 'Ballet des nations'," *Journal for Early Modern Cultural Studies* 13, 2 (Spring 2013): 3–23.

91 Foster, "Choreographing Empathy."

92 Kate van Orden, *Music, Discipline, and Arms in Early Modern France* (Chicago: The University of Chicago Press, 2005).

93 For a detailed description, see Sarah Cohen, *Art, Dance, and the Body*, 40.

94 Norbert Elias, *The Civilizing Process*, trans. Edmund Jephcott (Oxford: Blackwell Publishing, 1994); Georges Vigarello, "The Upward Training of the Body from the Age of Chivalry to Court Civility," in *Fragments for a History of the Human Body*, ed. Michel Feher, Ramona Naddaf, and Nadia Tazi, 3 vols. (New York: Zone, 1989), 2: 148–99.

95 "Plainte d'Anne-Catherine Desmares contre son mari Antoine-François Botot dit Dangeville, qui l'avait battue et injuriée (November 16, 1725)," reprinted in Émile Campardon, *Les Comédiens du roi de la troupe française pendant des deux derniers siècles* (Paris: Chez H. Champion, 1879). Botot-Dangeville's wife was the actress Catherine Desmares, sister of Charlotte Desmares, the one-time mistress of France's Regent and the mother of Maurepas's secretary Salleé. On Botot Dangeville as the possible choreographer, see Nathalie Rizzoni, "*Le Prince Pot à thé* de Caylus, de la porcelaine à la pantomime," in Quéro, ed., *Théâtre de société du comte de Caylus*, 457.

96 Susan Leigh Foster, "Introduction," in *Choreography and Narrative: Ballet's Staging of Story and Desire* (Bloomington and Indianapolis: Indiana University Press, 1996).

97 Jean-Baptiste du Halde, *Description [. . .] de l'Empire de la Chine*, translated into English as *The General History of China. Containing a Geographical, Historical, Chronological, Political and Physical Description of the Empire of China, Chinese-Tartary, Corea and Thibet*, 4 vols. (London: J. Watts, 1741), 3: 65.

98 Angela Kang, "Musical Chinoiserie" (PhD dissertation, University of Nottingham, UK, 2005).

99 Rose Pruiksma, "Of Dancing Girls and *Sarabandes*: Music, Dance, and Desire in Court Ballet, 1651–1669," *The Journal of Musicology* 35, 2 (2018): 145–82.

100 Mary Sheriff, *Enchanted Islands*, 8.

101 On these types of prints, see David Pullins, "Techniques of the Body: Viewing the Arts and Métiers of France from the Workshop of Nicolas I and Nicolas II de Larmessin," *Oxford Art Journal* 37, 2 (2014): 135–55; and Jones, *Shapely Bodies*, 15–17.

102 Mouat and Mouat, "European Perceptions of Chinese Culture."

103 Phil Chan, *Final Bow for Yellowface: Dancing Between Intention and Impact* (Brooklyn: Yellow Peril Press, 2020). See also https://www.yellowface.org/.

104 Pierre de Morand, *Correspondance littéraire de Nîmes*, quoted in Guo Tang, "De l'artifice au réalisme: L'évolution des 'chinoiseries' théâtrales dans la première moitié du 18e siècle," *Dix-huitième siècle* 49, 1 (2017): 653–54: "Les attitudes de magots que les danseurs tâchent d'imiter n'ont rien de flatteur. Ce sont des contorsions, des grimaces, des mines fort disgracieuses à voir. Ce ne sont que des pas extraordinaires, forcés, peu naturels [. . .] en un mot, c'est une frivolité qui ne peut que détruire pour cet art le bon gout qui nous restait, comme elle a détruit celui que l'on avait pour les autres arts."

105 Morand, *Correspondance littéraire*, quoted in Tang, "De l'artifice au réalisme," 655: "Nous verrons immanquablement des palanquins dans les rues de Paris. Il serait fort plaisant d'y voir aussi les hommes avec des moustaches à queue et des barbiches pendantes."

106 *Les Magots, parodie de "L'Orphelin de la Chine," en vers, en 1 acte* (Paris: Vve Delormel et fils, 1756). One printing claims the (anonymous) author to be "Boucher (officer au service de la Compagnie des Indes)." On the English adaptation of *L'Orphelin de la Chine* by Arthur Murphy, see Chi-ming Yang, *Performing China: Virtue: Commerce, and Orientalism in Eighteenth-Century England, 1660–1760* (Baltimore: Johns Hopkins University Press, 2011), chap. 4.

107 Jérôme de La Gorce, *Féeries d'opéra: Décors, machines et costumes en France 1645–1765* (Paris: Éditions du patrimoine, 1997), 132–33. I am grateful to Kate Tunstall for telling me about Algieri's maquette.

108 Amanda Moehlenpah, "'Les assemblées qu'elle occasionne': Danced Sociability in Eighteenth-Century France," *Eighteenth-Century Studies* 54, 3 (Spring 2021): 577–92.

109 Antoine Lilti has made a similar argument about the insularity of eighteenth-century salon culture; see *Le monde des salons: sociabilité et mondanité à Paris au XVIIIᵉ siècle* (Paris: Fayard, 2005). For debates about the "subversiveness" of masquerade, see Terry Castle, *Masquerade and Civilization: The Carnivalesque in Eighteenth-Century English Culture and Fiction* (Stanford: Stanford University Press, 1986).

110 Anne Anlin Cheng, "Monsters, Cyborgs, and Vases: Apparitions of the Yellow Woman," lecture presented to the Harvard Graduate School of Design, September 21, 2021. See also Cheng, "Ornamentalism"; and for *kintsugi*, see Christy Bartlett et al., *FlickWerk: The Aesthetics of Mended Japanese Ceramics* (Münster: Museum für Lackkunst and Ithaca: Herbert F. Johnson Museum of Art, 2008).

111 Jeff Ravel, "The Coachman's Bare Rump: An Eighteenth-Century French Cover-Up," *Eighteenth-Century Studies* 40, 2 (Winter 2007): 279–308. Ravel interestingly notes that the aristocrats involved later tried to deny or cover up the incident.

112 Ravel, "The Coachman's Bare Rump," 291. Rouillé was also related to the navy minister for whom the report about Charles de Caylus's activities as colonial governor was written.

113 Sue Peabody, *"There Are No Slaves In France": The Political Culture of Race and Slavery in the Ancien Régime* (New York: Oxford University Press, 1996).

114 Meredith Martin and Gillian Weiss, "Enslaved Muslims at the Sun King's Court," in *The Versailles Effect: Objects, Lives, and Afterlives of the Domaine*, ed. Mark Ledbury and Robert Wellington (London: Bloomsbury Visual Arts, 2020), chap. 10.

115 Saidiya Hartman, "Venus in Two Acts," *Small Axe* 26 (June 2008): 13.

J.B. Martin Inv. et Sculp.

Chinois.
Dans les Indes Galantes et autres Ballets.

A Paris chez Esnauts et Rapilly rue St. Jacques, à la Ville de Coutances. A.P.D.R.

PHIL CHAN

MY PORCELAIN SICKNESS

I met Meredith Martin when she attended a virtual talk I was giving at NYU. A leading art historian who specializes in eighteenth-century decorative arts and global trade, she approached me after my talk with an irresistible proposition—would I be interested in reimagining a baroque fantasy ballet about a Chinese sorcerer on my own terms as a contemporary Chinese American?

In the course of Meredith's research on porcelain, she came across references to a lost eighteenth-century pantomime ballet, the *Ballet des Porcelaines*, or *The Teapot Prince*. Created in 1739, not long after the Chinese secret for making true or hard-paste porcelain was discovered in Europe, the ballet can be interpreted as an allegory of West triumphing over East. Meredith briefly described the plot to me: a despotic Sorcerer rules over a "Blue Island," transforming his subjects and intruders with a flick of his wand into porcelain wares. A Prince is caught in his snares, only to be rescued by the Princess he loves. Together, they steal the Sorcerer's wand, and after they discover the secret of his magic, they turn him into a porcelain bobblehead.

Despite having only two eighteenth-century performances, the influence of the *Ballet des Porcelaines* trickled down into the work of subsequent artists as a way to represent Chinese people. The choreographer Marius Petipa, of *The Nutcracker* (1892) and *Swan Lake* (1895) fame, knew of the ballet, and seems to have referenced it in the final act of his own *Sleeping Beauty* (1890), which features a porcelain prince and two porcelain princesses.

Here is where Meredith saw the potential for her research to intersect with my advocacy. Along with New York City Ballet soloist Georgina "Gina" Pazcoguin, I am the co-founder of Final Bow for Yellowface (www.yellowface.org), which since 2017 has worked to improve how the international ballet community represents Asians on stage. What started with a conversation with New York City Ballet's then-Artistic Director Peter Martins has quickly garnered support from every major ballet company in America, as well as companies across Europe and Australia, through the signing of a simple pledge:

> I love ballet as an art form, and acknowledge that to achieve diversity among our artists, audiences, donors, students, volunteers, and staff requires inclusion. I am committed to eliminating outdated and offensive stereotypes of Asians (Yellowface) on our stages.

This year is the fifth anniversary of our work with Final Bow for Yellowface. At this point, every major American company has signed our pledge, as well as leading international companies like the UK's Royal Ballet, the National Ballet of Canada, and the Australian Ballet. In addition, we were cited in the Paris Opéra's recent

FIGURE 26

Jean-Baptiste Martin, "Chinois, dans *Les Indes galantes* et autres ballets," from *Galerie des modes et costumes français, dessinés d'après nature* (Paris, 1778–87). Colored engraving, 22 × 16.5 cm. Jerome Robbins Dance Division, The New York Public Library, Astor, Lenox and Tilden Foundations.

diversity report as a contributing factor in its decision to discontinue the use of blackface and yellowface on their stages.

I'm also approaching the *Ballet des Porcelaines* project with quite a bit of fresh historical context, having just finished a dance research fellowship in 2020 with The New York Public Library for the Performing Arts at Lincoln Center, where I looked at about one hundred Orientalist ballets from the 1700s to today. What I found was a very robust appetite in Europe for consuming and performing fantasies of Asian people. An Oriental setting allowed for all sorts of fantastic scenarios and taboo subject matter to be explored—literally sex, drugs, and rock and roll.

In the course of my research, I realized that Orientalism has been the greatest driver of innovation and creativity in many Western art forms. Think about it: a setting close to home must be rooted in some degree of cultural authenticity; if we live in France and the ballet is set in France, the costumes had better look French or else the audience will be disoriented and confused. But when telling stories about exotic peoples and places—and especially China, with which there was little actual contact

thin dance floor rolled over an outdoor concrete path. Or a raised platform between two antique urns. I am no stranger to site-specific work; one of my more avant-garde dance teachers growing up organized a show for us on a Hong Kong beach with the South China Sea as our set. I've never assumed that dance could take place only in a theater. However, with a baroque and modern dance vocabulary, a few conditions needed to be met to perform safely and with integrity. Flooring must be even, have some give, and not be slippery. Versatile footwear would have to be considered. The inclusion of virtuoso turns and jumps would have to be restrained.

The spaces for every venue would also be different, requiring a reconfiguration of the entire ballet at every new performance location. Knowing this from day one, I made the ballet components modular, and even made the individual dance phrases capable of being scaled up to include more traveling and movement if we have more space, or pared down if the stage is small, while still retaining all of the movement I wanted to include. These are all things that had to be considered when working outside of a rectangular proscenium stage with ideal conditions.

I'm happy with the final product, which is, like me, a fusion. I love seeing touches of my Chinese heritage dotting the movement landscape, and how the baroque divertissement feeling has been preserved. I feel like the ballet keeps a modern audience's attention and touches on themes relevant to us today, while offering a little glimpse into the past intentions of the original creators.

On Music

I wasn't quite sure at first how to approach imagining dances to score. My prior experience with baroque music consisted mostly of middle school cello and recorder recitals, and being dragged to early music concerts in Berkeley by my mother because she was dating a lute player. He owned a theorbo, a long-necked plucked lute that he called his giraffe, which he kept in a room with a special dehumidifier. He was very fussy about it. That was my general opinion about anything baroque—fussy.

The music for the *Ballet des Porcelaines* was intimidating at first. Brought to life after nearly three centuries via a recording by our wonderful musical directors, the harpsichordist Dongsok Shin and violinist Leah Gale Nelson, the rich colors and tones within the music began to emerge. Paired with the historical context provided by Meredith, I started to imagine not only what the original work might have looked like, but also what the intended impact might have been on the audience.

Listening to the score for the first time, I was struck by how pretty the music was, but was skeptical that it could convey some of the darker parts of the story, especially for a contemporary audience. I also wanted to break up the pacing: originally there was a longer prologue before the plot, and less character development once the story starts. While that balance might have satisfied a half-drunk eighteenth-century aristocratic audience, I felt it might leave an audience today feeling empty. Could we apply the same *kintsugi* approach to the musical score?

I called my friend Sugar Vendil, a proud second-generation Filinpinx American composer, who I knew would be perfect. Her work features complex melodies layered to create both a sense of magic and discomfort. She is also skilled at using nontraditional sounds, and describes her interest as an artist as lying "in the coexistence of equal-tempered and microtonal sounds." Plus, she's a dancer. I knew she would compose great "*kintsugi* music" for voice, breath, and the sounds of porcelain. Porcelain

to symbolize an eerie state of physical suspension. These transformed masked characters were living statues, brittle and grotesque.

There is also the addition of new pantomime in this reimagining, namely the central duet between the Prince and the Princess. In the original, there is very little exposition of the Princess transforming the Prince back into human form. I felt that for an audience today, there needed to be a more substantial and powerful dance for these two characters. The larger theme of the work is about being able to see each other with greater nuance, so I needed to make space for the two central characters to be able to express that.

I wanted to make a dance for the Princess who comes across her lover, resigns herself to the fact that despite using the magic wand, and even giving him True Love's Kiss, he is gone forever. She approaches him again, not to try to reawaken him, but this time to say goodbye. She wants to make a memory of him, of how he held her, of how she nestled against him. And by dropping her guard and dancing with him, she succeeds in bringing him back to life.

As we were making the *pas de deux* between the Princess and the frozen porcelain Prince, I kept encouraging Ying to slow down. "It looks like you're just picking stuff up at the grocery store," I teased. We had to actually write out dialogue to figure out the emotional journey of her character, and then layer on movement that reflected that.

> Have you ever visited a dying relative, and you go and hold their hand one more time? Or touch their hair, make a memory of how they smell and how they feel in your arms, before saying goodbye? That is the feeling I want to re-create in this duet.

No, this element wasn't in the original *Ballet des Porcelaines*, but I felt it rounded out the characters and brought the audience along emotionally in a way that wasn't possible with just the baroque score and pantomime alone. This was a big piece of *kintsugi* that I wanted to graft onto to the ballet today.

Reconstruction and Diversity

Many ballet revivals that look to the past for inspiration include a historical advisor, who helps frame the social context of when the ballet originally premiered and assists with ensuring the final work is a product of its historical time. As the porcelain sickness Patient Zero for the rest of us working on *The Teapot Prince*, Meredith provided countless points of historical reference at every twist and turn of the creative process. Watching us toy with a new concept or a different way of approaching a creative problem, Meredith would help with everything from supplying period-appropriate color palettes to shaping the identity of the characters based on actual historical figures (like our Augustus the Strong-inspired Sorcerer) to providing critical insight into the impact of the work on eighteenth-century audiences. Unlike the rigid corsets that conservative historians may put on a revival process, Meredith's approach gave us appropriate guardrails in order for us to tease out the heart of the fairy tale ballet. And our creative work is richer for it; the context she provided was able to set the ballet free.

I'm sure there will be purists who are disappointed that the time, energy, and resources spent on this reimagination weren't instead devoted to something that was closer to what the original eighteenth-century performance might have been. For the general public, though, I don't think too many people really care about reliving history exactly the way it was; we can't just say, "Hey this work is old and super racist, sorry if you're offended, but enjoy the show!" We have to recognize that, for the most part, people do not like to see centuries-old outsider fantasies that distort their culture.

A single, outdated, Eurocentric view of China in the original *Ballet des Porcelaines* doesn't work for people like us today, who consider ourselves citizens of the world. In the interconnected twenty-first century, your favorite food could be tacos, your favorite city might be Marrakech, and you might be a huge K-pop fan. You can visit anywhere in the world through a video available in the palm of your hand. Through the internet, we now have access to authentic expressions of each other's cultures in a way that was never previously possible in the entirety of human history.

Therefore, as an audience, we can't claim ignorance and enjoy fantasies of Cathay anymore—at a time when we very much need to see the realities of both the lived experiences of Asian Americans and the growing role of China on the geopolitical stage. We cannot afford to let coolie Chinamen caricatures or precious porcelain Princesses obscure the realities of how Asians are viewed both here at home and abroad. As we have seen in prior conflicts, whether with the internment of the Japanese after Pearl Harbor or the extermination of the Jews during the Holocaust, xenophobia rears its ugly head at the intersection of stereotypes and fear. As an artist, I cannot control the greater irrational fears we have about each other, but I can use the time that I have your attention to question the stereotypes that have been handed down to us through the centuries. This means we have to perform the ballet today differently than it was performed in the eighteenth century. We must reinterpret. As an Asian American, I can't afford not to.

Perhaps that is why I feel a certain sense of empowerment knowing that the movement of the ballet was mostly created in my dad's backyard while I was visiting him, dancing between two orange trees in his small rectangular refuge from the ugliness outside.

I am not only interested in finding new ways to tell old stories for today, but also supporting new stories to be made. Our iteration of the *Ballet des Porcelaines* encompasses both of these seemingly contradictory desires; hopefully we have not only stayed true to the shape and spirit of the original work, but have also allowed a new allegory to emerge that may ring truer for an audience today.

More broadly, I see this process—the work of making meaningful multiracial works for everyone, while still holding onto our specific tradition—as great creative uncharted territory ahead; as the greatest challenge facing performing artists and creative leaders in our multicultural societies today. But I also see this process as a huge wellspring of untapped creative potential that our generation has been waiting for. It is my hope that the *Ballet des Porcelaines* succeeds as my first attempt to encapsulate some of these ideals in practice.

CHARLOTTE VIGNON

CONJURING 1740

A Tale of Europe's Obsession with Porcelain

In 1739, when the influential comte de Caylus (1692–1765) wrote his ballet panto-mime *Le Prince Pot-à-Thé* (*The Teapot Prince*; also known as the *Ballet des Porcelaines*), the allure of porcelain was at its peak in Europe. Nonetheless, the ballet would be performed only twice, once in September 1739 and again in 1741, both times at the château of Morville near Paris. Each performance, according to Caylus's libretto, was meant to last "no more than a generous fifteen minutes."[1] As discussed by Mer-edith Martin in this volume, Caylus was a friend of the château's owner, Charles-Jean-Baptiste Fleuriau, comte de Morville (1686–1732), an important collector of Asian porcelain and also, as France's foreign minister, a promoter of trade with Asia.

Not unlike Gabrielle-Suzanne de Villeneuve's *Beauty and the Beast*, published in 1740, Caylus's story involves star-crossed lovers, an evil spell, and metamorphosis. A prince in search of his beloved is held captive on an exotic island by a diaboli-cal sorcerer who has turned its inhabitants into porcelain, a fate that also befalls the prince, who is transformed into a teapot. The prince is unrecognizable to his lover until the two of them break the spell, at which point they find each other. Caylus's story seems to reflect on the European desire not only to obtain porcelain but also to possess the secrets of making it, a kind of alchemy that required the four elements—Earth, Air, Water, and Fire, all alluded to in his ballet—and mul-tiple chemical processes to become what was known to Europeans at the time as "white gold." The earth element is kaolin, a naturally white clay discovered first in China during the Yuan Dynasty (1279–1368) in a village near Jingdezhen, and then found several centuries later in Europe, first in Saxony and later in France near Limoges. Water must be added to the mixture of raw materials, including feldspar and quartz, to obtain the porcelain paste. Once shaped, the pieces must be dried by air before being fired at a very high temperature, after which they become white, translucent, and fully vitrified—an impermeable material that, like magic, reflects light instead of absorbing it.

The Caylus tale is an early literary work by this polymath who later published several collections of fairy tales, among them *Féeries nouvelles* (*New Enchantments*, 1741), *Contes orientaux* (*Oriental Tales*, 1743), and *Cinq contes de fées* (*Five Fairy Tales*, 1745), as well as many important texts on the arts, including one on the chemical com-position of Greek ceramics (suggesting that he shared some of the same scientific obsessions as the porcelain manufacturers discussed in this essay).[2] As a young no-bleman initially destined for a military career, Caylus chose instead a life devoted

FIGURE 31

Chinese musicians, c. 1755–56. Model attributed to Joseph Willems, Chelsea manufactory, soft-paste porcelain decorated in polychrome enamels, 36.8 x 36.8 x 37.1 cm. The Metropolitan Museum of Art, Gift of Irwin Untermeyer, 1964 (64.101.474).

to art and literature. From an early age, he was a great traveler, journeying to Great Britain, the Netherlands, Germany, and Italy, as well as farther afield to Constantinople and Greece, where he began his study of antiquity—a prelude to his becoming an avid collector of antiquities and a preeminent antiquarian. In Paris, he frequented literary salons and was part of the circle of the powerful, immensely rich financier and art collector Pierre Crozat (1661–1740). There he met and became friends with the painters Antoine Watteau (1684–1721) and Rosalba Carriera (1675–1757), as well as the influential engraver, art dealer, and collector Pierre-Jean Mariette (1694–1774).

With the contemporary revival of the *Ballet des Porcelaines*—which, like *Sleeping Beauty*, is emerging after almost three centuries of silence—I would like to take you back in time, to about 1740, and to the European nations at the heart of the quest to uncover the secret of producing porcelain. Several are also the same countries where performances of the *Ballet des Porcelaines* are scheduled to be held in summer 2022—Great Britain, Italy, and France. Because of its foundational role in unlocking this secret, the Meissen manufactory in Germany will also be considered, as will the American China manufactory, since the reimagined ballet was created in the United States and premiered there (at The Metropolitan Museum of Art) in December 2021.

But first, I want to set the clock back to an even earlier moment, sometime before the fifteenth century, when a very few pieces of the porcelain that had been manufactured in China since the seventh century began to reach Europe from Asia. The prized possession of a few discerning European princes, Chinese porcelain was not only valued for its rarity and beauty but was also an object of fascination for the mysteries surrounding its manufacture.[3] By the mid-sixteenth century, with the landing of Portuguese ships on the south coast of China several decades earlier, Chinese porcelain began to reach Europe with more regularity. By the early seventeenth century, a great quantity of Chinese porcelains of varied quality arrived in Europe as a result of the tea trade between European companies and East and South

FIGURE 32 Five-part "Elements" garniture, 1742. Johann Joachim Kaendler and Johann Friedrich Eberlein (modellers), Meissen manufactory, hard-paste porcelain, 84 cm (central vase). Porzellansammlung, Dresden (PE 104 a, b, PE 101, PE 107 a, b, PE 7789, PE 3735 a, b). © Porzellansammlung, Staatliche Kunstsammlungen Dresden. Photo by Herbert Jaeger.

Asia, including the mighty Dutch East India Company (Vereenigde Oost Indische Compagnie, or VOC), established in 1602. After 1660, Japanese porcelain began to reach Europe, though in much smaller quantities than Chinese porcelain: no fewer than four million pieces of the latter were imported between 1700 and 1705 into London alone.[4] In Dresden during the same period, whole cargos of porcelain arrived in the city nearly every day.[5]

From the mid-seventeenth century to the mid-eighteenth century, Asian porcelains were displayed in aristocratic houses all over Europe, arranged on mantelpieces, chests of drawers, and other flat surfaces, as well as on walls—sometimes on brackets that were gilded or that imitated lacquer and bamboo.[6] Asian porcelain became a revealing expression of an owner's taste and social status. Over the years, European porcelain was gradually added to these Asian porcelain displays; whereas some were simple imitations of Asian models, others were European inventions.

Parallel to the history of porcelain imported from Asia was that of the quest for the formula of the porcelain paste, the arcanum, as well as the secrets of the firing process, so that porcelain could be produced in Europe. This was a tale of passion and obsession, ambition and pride, persistence and luck. In time, the European kings, princes, and entrepreneurs who were so determined to uncover these secrets succeeded and were able to create beautiful porcelains, among them those produced in Florence in the second half of the sixteenth century under the patronage of Francesco I de' Medici (1541–1587). However, this kind of soft-paste porcelain was made without kaolin, the white clay essential for producing true or hard-paste Asian-type porcelain. Producing porcelain equal to that made in Asia was finally achieved by Augustus II (1694–1733), Elector of Saxony and later King of Poland, who was known as Augustus the Strong. Augustus's precarious financial situation and attendant thirst for gold led him to imprison the German alchemist Johann Friedrich Böttger (1682–1719) in order to control his experiments. During Böttger's attempts to make gold, he discovered the secret for producing true porcelain.[7] Böttger's goal of creating "extraordinary things"[8] in porcelain was achieved in January 1710, when Augustus the Strong founded a porcelain manufactory in Dresden, the seat of the Saxon court.

So determined was the king to keep the formula a secret that, later that same year, he relocated his factory to Albrechtsburg, a secure medieval clifftop castle in Meissen. Between 1710 and 1740, the Royal Meissen manufactory led the ceramic industry in Europe, both scientifically and artistically, producing hard-paste porcelain vases, tableware, teapots, cups, figures, groups, and life-size animals. Many were reproductions of Asian wares, while others were embellished in a style developed at Meissen by the talented Viennese painter Johann Gregorius Höroldt (1696–1777). Höroldt's distinctive decorations included colorful miniature scenes—often in a style later termed *chinoiserie*, depicting life in China as imagined by Europeans—set in reserves and framed with ornaments. The technical and artistic perfection reached by the Meissen manufactory is embodied by an extraordinary set of three white vases and two pitchers depicting allegories of the four elements in low and high relief; it was meant to be offered in the early 1740s as a diplomatic gift from Augustus III (1696–1763), son of Augustus the Strong, to France's King Louis XV (Fig. 32).[9]

The Triumph of Meissen (1710 to the Present), the First Producer of Hard-Paste Porcelain in Europe

A Producer of Hard-Paste Porcelain in Venice: The Vezzi Manufactory (1720–1727)

In 1740, no porcelain was being made in Venice. Twenty years earlier, however, a certain Giovanni Vezzi (b. 1687) founded in the Serenissima the third European manufactory to produce hard-paste porcelain, after Meissen and the du Paquier manufactory founded in Vienna in 1718.[10] The Vezzi factory was in operation for only seven years; it was not until much later, in 1763, that another porcelain manufactory—the Cozzi factory—would be established in Venice.

Giovanni Vezzi was joined in his venture by two other Venetians, Giovanni Marco Norbis and Giovanni Maria Santinelli, but it was the arrival of the German gilder and arcanist Christoph Conrad Hunger (c. 1717-c. 1748) that changed the game. Hunger had previously worked at the Meissen manufactory, where he learned secret recipes for fabricating hard-paste porcelain pieces, as well as tricks for successfully firing them. He was recruited by Giovanni's father, Francesco Vezzi (1651–1740), who provided the financial backing for his son's project and was counting on its commercial success. The two met in Vienna, where Hunger was working for Claudius Innocentius du Paquier (1705–1751), who had used his diplomatic connections to lure Hunger and several other key figures from Meissen two years earlier. In 1724, after just four years in Venice, Hunger returned to Meissen, at which point Giovanni Vezzi became the sole owner, although financial difficulties forced him to close the factory in 1727.

Not surprisingly, the porcelains produced at the Vezzi manufactory were similar to those made at Meissen and du Paquier. For a while, before kaolin was found in Tretto in the province of Vicenza, all three factories used the same kaolin from Schneeberg, in the Vosges mountains. Vezzi shapes and decorations were inspired by those made at Meissen and du Paquier, with a characteristic sense of sculptural animation and a touch of the Venetian decorative tradition mixed in. Of the fewer than two hundred pieces of Vezzi porcelain that are thought to have survived today, a significant number are teapots decorated with *chinoiserie* figures and motifs (Fig. 33).

FIGURE 33

Teapot, c. 1720–27. Vezzi manufactory, hard-paste porcelain, 12.1 cm. The Metropolitan Museum of Art, Rogers Fund, 1906 (06.362a, b).

By 1740, a number of porcelain factories had been established in Europe, primarily in France, Germany, and Italy. However, their production was exclusively soft-paste—like the sixteenth-century Medici wares—not the highly prized hard-paste porcelain made in Asia and at the Meissen and Vezzi manufactories. The composition of soft-paste porcelain, which includes a mixture of fine white clay and ground glass, cannot withstand temperatures above 1100°C without cracking. Therefore, soft-paste pieces, though white, are rarely translucent and never fully vitrified like hard-paste porcelain, which is fired at higher temperatures of 1250–1400° C. Although the recipes for soft-paste porcelain varied depending on time and place, and were typically inconsistent even within a single factory, soft-paste objects are usually warmer in tone, slightly ivory, and thicker than those made of hard paste. Nonetheless, it can be challenging for a non-expert to differentiate one from the other.

The development of porcelain manufactories in Europe during the first half of the eighteenth century coincided with changes in dining customs and the introduction of hot beverages. Up until the 1730s, when the Meissen manufactory began producing unified dinner services with coordinated decoration, wealthy Europeans had dined on services that combined ceramics of various provenances with wares made in other media like silver. Existing porcelain manufactories picked up on the fashion for coordinated services, while new porcelain manufactories were founded to respond to this consumer demand. Soft- or hard-paste porcelain also began to be considered as the ideal medium for the consumption of tea, chocolate, and coffee: beverages that became popular among the European aristocracy from the mid-seventeenth century, fueling not only the fabrication and circulation of porcelain but also colonial and imperial expansion, themes that are latent in Caylus's ballet. The growing demand for vessels with which to consume these drinks led European porcelain manufactories to step up their production of cups and saucers, as well as tea, chocolate, and coffee pots and sets.

European Manufactories
of Soft-Paste Porcelain

In France, the well-guarded formula for producing soft-paste porcelain was discovered in 1673 by Louis Poterat (1641–1696). He was the oldest son of Edme Poterat, a prominent *faiencier* (maker of tin-glazed earthenware) in Rouen who, during the next two decades, developed a small production of soft-paste porcelain decorated almost exclusively with blue and white. In 1674, Pierre Chicaneau, a faience painter from Rouen, took over a faience manufactory located on the banks of the Seine in Saint-Cloud. This was near Paris and the château de Saint-Cloud, the primary residence of Philip, duc d'Orléans (1640–1701), the younger brother of Louis XIV and a great collector of Asian porcelains. A report written in 1702 states: "Pierre Chicaneau père, having devoted himself for several years to the production of faience and having attained a high degree of perfection in this work, sought further to advance his learning, to the point of discovering the secret of producing true porcelain."[11] But Chicaneau died in 1677 without finding the recipe to produce either soft- or hard-paste porcelain. By the mid-1690s, his wife and children, aided by the Poterat family, began producing soft-paste wares at Saint-Cloud. Like the Poterat factory, they first produced primarily small objects—pomade pots, snuffboxes, knife handles, cups and saucers, small vases—that imitated Chinese blue-and-white porcelain.[12]

The Saint-Cloud Manufactory
(1674–1766) near Paris

However, with the patronage of the duc d'Orléans, the Saint-Cloud manufactory quickly achieved commercial success and gained European recognition.

When the British scientist Martin Lister (1638–1712) visited the manufactory in 1698, he said: "I confess I could not distinguish between the Pots made there, and the finest China Ware I ever saw."[13] By the 1700s, Saint-Cloud was producing more varied and ambitious works: ewers, basins, bowls, and cream jars for the morning toilette, along with tableware, writing cases, cups and saucers, tea and coffee pots, and chocolate services. While still mostly ornamented with the factory's characteristic cobalt-blue decoration, they no longer copied Chinese porcelain

FIGURE 34

Two actors mounted as candelabra, c. 1730–40. Saint-Cloud manufactory, soft-paste porcelain decorated in polychrome enamels and gold, gilt bronze mounts, 36.8 cm. The Metropolitan Museum of Art, The Jack and Belle Linsky Collection, 1982 (1982. 60.254).

but employed European motifs instead. As a result of its success, in 1702 the factory received a royal privilege to better facilitate production. Around 1720–30, the Saint-Cloud manufactory created polychrome works directly inspired by contemporary Chinese *famille verte* and *famille rose* porcelain, as well as Japanese porcelain in the Kakiemon and Imari styles.

During the following decade, the factory added to its repertoire the production of white porcelain with a relief decor, a style inspired by Chinese porcelain. It also started to create small figures that were often mounted in gilt bronze to form *objets d'art* or simply to enhance their status and value. One pair of figurines represents two European actors dressed as Chinese characters mounted as candelabras

(Fig. 34). Their identification as "Chinese" is evidenced by the hat and facial hair of the male actor, as well as the pattern of the costumes worn by both figures, which derives from motifs and colors found on Japanese export porcelain. The production of such figures was likely a response by the Saint-Cloud manufactory to the popularity of theatrical events with *chinoiserie* themes that were taking place in Paris and its environs around this time, including the comic opera *La Princesse de la Chine*, performed at the Foire Saint-Laurent in 1729; a *Divertissement chinois* staged at the Théâtre de l'Hôtel de Bourgogne in 1737; and, of course, the *Ballet des Porcelaines*.[14]

The formula for producing soft-paste porcelain was a well-kept secret at the Saint-Cloud manufactory until Louis-Henri (1692–1740)—duc de Bourbon and prince de Condé, grandson of Louis XIV, and, like Augustus the Strong and the duc d'Orléans before him, a passionate collector of Asian porcelain—decided that he too should own a porcelain manufactory. It was to be established near his château in Chantilly, approximately sixty miles north of Paris. Around 1730, the prince de Condé lured the services of Cicaire Cirou (1700–1755), who had worked as a *faiencier* and painter on porcelain at the Saint-Cloud manufactory from 1722–28. In 1729, Cirou also collaborated with the physician, chemist, and naturalist René Antoine Ferchault de Réaumur (1683–1757), who had been interested in the production of porcelain since 1717.[15] Despite his background and work with Ferchault de Réaumur, Cirou developed only a grayish porcelain paste at Chantilly that had to be covered with a tin glaze in order to give the pieces, after firing, the desired white appearance.[16]

It was only after 1738, with Claude-Humbert Gérin's discovery that the addition of alum to the paste made it whiter, that the Chantilly manufactory was able to produce perfectly white soft-paste porcelain (an achievement that coincided with the creation of the *Ballet des Porcelaines*). Gérin left Chantilly in 1740, taking his recipe with him to the newly founded Vincennes manufactory.[17] But this did not prevent the Chantilly manufactory from being successful. Quite the opposite. It gave the early Chantilly porcelain pieces a unique cool, opaque white surface that intrigued even Augustus the Strong; in January 1733, he gave a few Chantilly plates to his chemists and artisans at the Meissen manufactory so they could try to figure out the recipe for the Chantilly pieces.[18] And on October 5, 1735, the Chantilly manufactory was granted a twenty-year royal privilege to produce "porcelains of all kinds of colors, types, shapes, and sizes, imitating the porcelain of Japan."[19]

This specific artistic direction reflects both the patron's taste and the style already developed at the factory since its foundation. Indeed, from 1730 until 1740, when the factory lost its main patron, Louis-Henri de Bourbon-Condé, the Chantilly manufactory produced pieces with Kakiemon decoration after Japanese models almost exclusively. The rarity of original Japanese porcelain in Europe excited passionate collectors of Asian porcelain like Augustus the Strong and the prince de Condé, who at his death owned approximately seventeen hundred pieces of Asian ceramics, many of which were Japanese porcelains.[20] Both men naturally encouraged their porcelain manufactories to produce faithful imitations of Japanese pieces from their own collections. In the 1730s, the Chantilly manufactory also produced numerous small figures called *pagodes* and *magots*, eighteenth-century French terms for Asian

The Chantilly Manufactory (1730–1800), North of Paris

FIGURE 35

Potpourri vase in the shape of a *magot*, c. 1735–40. Chantilly manufactory, tin-glazed soft-paste porcelain decorated in polychrome enamels, 16.5 cm. Sèvres–Manufacture et musée nationaux, MNC18317. Photo © RMN-Grand Palais (Sèvres–Manufacture et musée nationaux) / Martine Beck-Coppola.

figures and figure groups. Left white or painted with polychrome decoration, they were often made into objects like clocks or potpourri vases, and they feature prominently in the fairy tale that inspired the *Ballet des Porcelaines*, entitled *Prince Perinet, or the Origin of Pagodes* (Fig. 35). (For more on pagods and *magots* and their significance with regard to Caylus's ballet, see Meredith Martin's essay in this volume.)

Despite these artistic and commercial successes, neither the Saint-Cloud nor Chantilly manufactory was able to withstand the competition presented by the Vincennes manufactory. Founded in 1740, a year after the *Ballet des Porcelaines* was performed for the first time, it was transferred to Sèvres sixteen years later and placed in 1759 under the patronage of Louis XV (1710–1774) and his mistress, Madame de Pompadour (1721–1764).

The Vincennes-Sèvres Manufactory (1740 to the Present) Near Paris

In 1740, Claude-Humbert Gérin left the Chantilly manufactory—where, a few years earlier, he had improved the whiteness of its porcelain paste—to establish a manufactory in Vincennes, just east of Paris. He was quickly joined in his new venture by the brothers Gilles and Robert Dubois, who had worked with him at Chantilly, Gilles as a modeler and Robert as a thrower. The departure in 1740 of these three key figures from Chantilly was probably related to the death of the prince de Condé in January of that year. By losing its main protector, the Chantilly manufactory's future became uncertain, and this encouraged others in France to try to establish their own factories.[21] The most well-connected among them were Philibert Orry de Vignory (1689–1747), controller-general of finances and director general of the arts, royal manufactories, and *Bâtiments du Roi* (the king's buildings), and his half-brother, Jean-Louis Henri Orry de Fulvy (1703–1751), *Commissaire du Roi auprès de la Compagnie des Indes* (the king's commissioner of the French East India Company). In 1737, Orry de Fulvy took over the position of *intendant des finances* from Jean-Jacques Amelot de Chaillou, a member of the amateur theater group that created and performed the *Ballet des Porcelaines*. Astute economists and politicians, the Orry brothers became interested in the production of porcelain in France as a way to limit its importation from Asia and Saxony. With their support, in 1740 Gérin and the Dubois brothers were able to set up a workshop and laboratory in one of the towers of the old royal château in Vincennes, where "they continued to experiment and made a few pieces that they sold secretly in Paris."[22]

Thanks to the Orry brothers, the factory received ten thousand *livres* from the royal budget, probably without the approval of Louis XV. Interestingly, between 1712 and 1722, their uncle, Father Louis-François Orry, administrator and treasurer of the Jesuit missions to China and India, had received from Francois-Xavier d'Entrecolles (1664–1741), a French Jesuit priest in China, a famous series of letters in which he described the Chinese techniques or "secrets" for manufacturing porcelain at Jingdezhen. Members of the Orry family would have had some kind of government or social connection with the comte de Morville in his capacity as foreign minister, as well as with the comte de Caylus, and it is interesting to speculate that their activities may have been evoked in some way by the ballet.

In 1741, Fulvy decided to finance the new enterprise and moved the manufactory to a larger space, still within the château de Vincennes, and hired five painters, seven sculptors, one thrower, and a certain François Gravant to assist Gérin.

In 1743, Gérin left the Vincennes manufactory after Gravant learned his recipes. His exit was followed the same year by that of Robert Dubois, and the following year by Gilles Dubois'.[23] Despite the departures of these key members of the manufactory, the young French company flourished, largely thanks to the extraordinary whiteness of Gérin's paste. In July 1745, Vincennes was granted a royal patent that gave it the exclusive right to produce "Meissen-like porcelain painted and gilded with human figures" for a twenty-year period.[24] From then on, the manufactory was designated as "royal," meaning that it was under the protection of the king of France, and each piece was signed with two interlaced *L*'s for Louis XV. The same summer of 1745, Madame de Pompadour became the official mistress (*maîtresse-en-titre*) of Louis XV. She and the king took a particular interest in the manufactory, which in 1756 was moved to specially constructed buildings in the town of Sèvres, halfway between the royal châteaux of the Tuileries and Versailles, and near Madame de Pompadour's château at Bellevue. Three years later, Louis XV became the factory's principal stockholder.

Under the patronage of Madame de Pompadour and Louis XV, Sèvres became the preeminent soft-paste porcelain factory in Europe. This triumph was due in part to the hiring of such renowned artists as the painter François Boucher (1703–1770) and Jean-Claude Duplessis (1699–1774), goldsmith to the king. Duplessis provided highly original models and designs such as the so-called Duplessis vase with two elephant heads, which evokes an exotic Eastern land more than referencing a specific Asian porcelain prototype (Fig. 36). Also key to the manufactory's reputation was the exclusive right it had to use gold decoration and a rich palette of colors developed by the chemist Jean Hellot (1685–1766), an eminent member of the Academy of Sciences who was continually inventing new colors and refining existing ones. In 1752, for example, Hellot created *bleu lapis*, a dark blue background color inspired by Chinese porcelain with powder-blue decoration—a technical innovation that greatly contributed to the factory's reputation and success.[25]

Due to their high cost, pieces from the French royal porcelain manufactory were owned only by the wealthy. Commissioned or purchased either at the manufactory or in the lavish Parisian shops of celebrated *merchands-merciers* (merchants of luxury goods) like Lazare Duvaux (c. 1703–1758), Vincennes and Sèvres porcelain was often presented as a gift to French courtiers or to foreign dignitaries, including the Qianlong emperor (1711–1799).

The establishment in 1743 of a soft-paste porcelain manufactory in Capodimonte outside of Naples was also the result of royal patronage. In 1738, Charles III (1716–1788), King of Naples, married Maria Amalia of Saxony (1724–1760), the granddaughter of Meissen's founder Augustus the Strong. Although we know the new queen brought Meissen porcelain to Naples as part of her dowry, her involvement in her husband's own efforts to produce porcelain in Naples is unclear.[26] By 1737, a year before their wedding, Charles III had already established the Neapolitan Tapestry manufactory and the pietre dure workshops at San Carlo, bringing grand economic and artistic plans to a city and a kingdom that he had conquered just three years earlier.[27] His marriage to Maria Amalia certainly would have encouraged him to found or develop his own porcelain factory.

FIGURE 36

Jean-Claude Duplessis, Elephant-head vase, c. 1758. Sèvres manufactory, soft-paste porcelain decorated in polychrome enamels and gold, 39.2 × 26.2 × 15.9 cm. The Metropolitan Museum of Art, Gift of Samuel H. Kress Foundation, 1958 (58.75.91a, b).

Real Fabbrica di Capodimonte (1743–1759) in Naples

It is not known when the Neapolitan search for the arcanum started or when firing experiments began, but the key chemists, artists, and artisans who contributed to the foundation of the porcelain factory arrived in Naples around 1735, at the same time as their king. The chemists Livio Vittorio Schepers and his son Gaetano came from Pisa to experiment on the formula for creating porcelain paste. Hoping first to obtain the recipes and raw materials from Saxony, the Veneto, or other manufactories, they confronted only well-guarded secrets and so had to find their own quarries and invent their own paste. After multiple failed experiments, they managed to create the glassy porcelain paste with high feldspar content that is characteristic of the Capodimonte manufactory. Production started sometime between 1740 and 1743, when the soft-paste manufactory was officially founded on the grounds of the royal château in Capodimonte. It quickly became one of the most successful porcelain manufactories in Europe.[28]

In September 1744, Giovanni Caselli proudly wrote that Gaetano Schepers's "formula was producing beautiful porcelain [. . .] the pieces have come out beautifully and with perfect colors and brightness so they are not inferior to Saxon porcelain."[29] The colors and painted decoration were the responsibility of Giovanni Caselli (d. 1753), a painter from Parma who became the first director of the Neapolitan factory. At Capodimonte, he developed very delicate painted decorations influenced by the French artist Antoine Watteau and the Italian painter Pietro Longhi. He was joined in this endeavor by the Florentine sculptor Giuseppe Gricci (c. 1700–1770), who created models for religious groups, as well as smaller figures that depict secular subjects drawn from the *commedia dell'arte* and from daily life. The latter includes a famous series of Neapolitan street criers, *Le voci di Napoli* (Fig. 37), a subject also favored and explored by the comte de Caylus.

During the early years of the Capodimonte factory, Meissen porcelain was a strong influence, especially for tableware. The Italian artists and artisans were inspired by Maria Amalia's personal porcelain collection, including a famous monochrome green service with scenes after Watteau that she brought with her from Saxony, as well as Meissen pieces modeled on Asian prototypes. However, the soft paste of the Neapolitan factory differed radically from Saxon hard paste, prompting the Italians to develop their own distinctive decorative styles, including still-life compositions after contemporary Neapolitan artists.[30] In the late 1750s, Maria Amalia once again influenced Capodimonte production by commissioning a porcelain room known as the "Chinese Cabinet of Queen Maria Amalia" and as the *Salottino di porcellana* (see Sarah Kozlowski and Sylvain Bellenger's essay in this volume). Created at the Palace of Portici between 1757 and 1759, the queen's boudoir was entirely covered with mirrors and white porcelain panels decorated in high relief with polychrome foliage, figures of monkeys and birds, Asian figures, and *chinoiserie* scenes, all conceived by Guiseppe Gricci. Despite the extremely high level of technical and artistic achievement this room embodied, the manufactory closed the same year it was finished, when Charles and Maria Amalia left Naples for Madrid so that Charles could assume his new role as king of Spain. They brought with them many of the Capodimonte artisans and some eighty-eight tons of equipment to found the new Buen Retiro porcelain manufactory.

Most of the porcelain factories established in Europe in the first half of the eighteenth century were supported by royal or noble patrons, who provided the financial support necessary to undertake experiments on paste and glazes and assumed the risk of launching companies that rarely operated at a profit. As a result, these factories' early productions reflected the tastes of their patrons, often avid collectors of Asian ceramics. English porcelain factories, by contrast, were not backed by royal or noble patrons but were instead founded as commercial enterprises. In order to become financially viable as quickly as possible, they produced functional wares and decorative objects for a wide market.

The earliest English porcelain factory was founded in 1744 in the fashionable London suburb of Chelsea by Nicolas Sprimont (1716–1771), a Huguenot newly established in Great Britain.[31] Two years earlier, Sprimont had arrived in London from Liège. Born into a family of goldsmiths, he was a successful silversmith and designer who made (or collaborated on) some of the most important silver works fabricated in England in the mid-eighteenth century, but who then decided to embark on the riskier business of porcelain production. This he did with the assistance of Charles Gouyn (d. 1785), a French Huguenot from Dieppe.[32] It is not clear how Sprimont uncovered the formulas for Chelsea's porcelain pastes and glazes, but as soon as he established the factory, it began making high-quality soft-paste porcelain with a glassy appearance. Chelsea wares were remarkable for their coveted whiteness, which was obtained by adding a considerable amount of lead to the paste and glaze.[33] Nevertheless, this feat did not prevent Sprimont, an astute businessman, from continuing to experiment with ways to improve the quality of

The Chelsea Manufactory (1744–1784) Outside of London

FIGURE 39

Installation view, *Porcelain, No Simple
Matter: Arlene Shechet and the Arnhold Collection*,
The Frick Collection, New York, 2016–17.
Courtesy of Arlene Shechet. Photo by Michael
Bodycomb. © The Frick Collection.

The fascination for porcelain persists today, and the limits and possibilities of the medium continue to be explored by contemporary artists around the world. Their enthusiasm is no doubt prompted by a desire to work with raw materials and to experiment with pastes and glazes, much like the chemists and alchemists who contributed to the founding of porcelain manufactories in eighteenth-century Europe. Upon their initial experiences working with porcelain, many artists become seduced by the magic of this extraordinarily malleable medium, which allows for objects to be made in all kinds of shapes and forms and with an infinite variety of decoration, until the pieces are fired and their appearance fixed with colors that never fade. Contemporary artists like Jean Girel, Jessica Harrison, and Arlene Shechet have responded to the long, rich history of the medium by sculpting pieces influenced by porcelain made since the seventh century in China and later in Europe (Fig. 39). But artists like Ni Haifeng, who uses his own body as a medium—presenting himself as a "Made in China" export as a way to comment both on the early modern Chinese/Dutch porcelain trade and its economic resonances in later eras—are also intrigued by porcelain's unique mobility and cross-cultural associations.[39] They create artworks that engage the politics of the porcelain trade as well as the obsession to produce it, continuing an ongoing dialogue with Asia and this magical medium that began many centuries ago.

1 See Christine Jones's annotated translation of the libretto in this volume.

2 Anne Claude de Tubières-Grimoard de Pestels de Lévis, comte de Caylus, *Contes*, ed. Julie Boch (Paris: Champion, 2005). See also Irène Aghion, ed., *Caylus mécène du roi. Collectionner les Antiquités au XVIIIe siècle* (Paris: Institut national d'histoire de l'art, 2002); and A.M. Pollard, "Letters from China: A History of the Origins of the Chemical Analysis of Ceramics," *Ambix* 62, 1 (2015): 50–71.

3 Stéphane Castelluccio, *Le goût pour les porcelains de Chine et du Japon à Paris aux XVIIe-XVIIIe siècles* (Saint-Rémy-en-l'Eau: Éditions Monelle Hayot, 2013), 15–16.

4 Tessa Murdoch, "Les cabinets de porcelaines," in *Pagodes et Dragons. Exotisme et fantaisie dans l'Europe rococo, 1720–1770*, ed. Georges Brunel, exh. cat. (Paris: Musée Cernuschi, 2007), 45.

5 Edmund de Waal, *The White Road: A Pilgrimage of Sorts* (London: Chatto & Windus, 2015), 155.

6 Murdoch, "Les cabinets de porcelaines."

7 On Johann Friedrich Böttger and his discovery of the formula for hard-paste porcelain, see Otto Walcha, *Meissen Porcelain* (New York: Putnam Pub Group, 1981), 15–47; Ingelore Menzhausen, *Early Meissen Porcelain in Dresden* (New York: Thames and Hudson, 1990), 10–13; Pietsch Ulrich and Claudia Banz, eds., *Triumph of the Blue Swords: Meissen Porcelain for Aristocracy and Bourgeoisie 1710–1815*, exh. cat. (Dresden: Staatliche Kunstsammlungen, Porzellansammlung; Leipzig: E. A. Seeman, 2010), 14–15; Martin Eberle, ed., *Das Rote Gold: Die Sammlung Böttgersteinzeug auf Schloss Friedenstein Gotha* (Gotha: Stiftung Schloss Friedenstein Gotha, 2011), 11–17; Ute Däberitz and Martin Eberle, eds., *Das weiße Gold: Die Sammlung Meissener Porzellan des 18. Jahrhunderts auf Schloss Friedenstein Gotha* (Gotha: Stiftung Schloss Friedenstein Gotha, 2012), 15–18; Jeffrey Munger, *European Porcelain in The Metropolitan Museum of Art* (New York: The Metropolitan Museum of Art; New Haven and London: Yale University Press, 2018), 46–48, 52–54; Edmund de Waal and Charlotte Vignon, *Gouthière's Candelabra* (New York and London: The Frick Collection in association with D. Giles Limited, 2019), 26–31. Janet Gleeson, *The Arcanum: The Extraordinary True Story* (London: Bantam, 1998), and Edmund de Waal, *The White Road*, 113–211, both tell the same story in a more novelistic way for a general audience.

8 Menzhausen, *Early Meissen Porcelain in Dresden*, 11.

9 Pietsch Ulrich and Theresa Witting, eds., *Fascination of Fragility: Masterpieces of European Porcelain*, exh. cat. (Leipzig: E.A. Seemann and Dresden: Staatliche Kunstsammlungen Dresden, 2010), 28; Jeffrey Munger and Selma Schwartz, "Gifts of Meissen Porcelain to the French Court, 1728–50," in *Fragile Diplomacy: Meissen Porcelain for European Courts ca. 1710–63*, ed. Maureen Cassidy-Geiger, exh. cat. (New Haven and London: Published for The Bard Graduate Center by Yale University Press, 2007), 156–58.

10 Andreina d'Agliano, "The Vezzi Porcelain Factory in Venice," in Pietsch and Witting, *Fascination of Fragility*, 65–66. For more on the du Paquier manufactory, which I have left out of this text since the *Ballet des Porcelaines* is not scheduled to be performed in Vienna, see Meredith Chilton, ed., *Fired by Passion: Vienna Baroque Porcelain of Claudius Innocentius du Paquier* (Hartford: Melinda and Paul Sullivan Foundation for the Decorative Arts and Stuttgart: Arnoldsche Art Publishers, 2009).

11 Bertrand Rondot, "The Saint-Cloud Porcelain Factory," in Pietsch and Witting, *Fascination of Fragility*, 43.

12 Bertrand Rondot, ed., "The Saint-Cloud Porcelain Manufactory: Between Innovation and Tradition," in *Discovering the Secrets of Soft-Paste Porcelain at The Saint-Cloud Manufactory, ca. 1690–1766*, exh. cat. (New Haven, CT: Yale University Press for the Bard Graduate Studies in the Decorative Arts, New York, 1999), 19, 264; Jeffrey Munger, *European Porcelain*, 138.

13 Rondot, "The Saint-Cloud Porcelain Factory," in Pietsch and Witting, *Fascination of Fragility*, 43.

14 Clare Le Corbeiller, "Saint-Cloud and the 'Goust de Raphaël'," in *Discovering the Secrets*, 29; Munger, *European Porcelain*, 146–48, no. 45. On Chinese-themed performances, see Guo Tang, "De l'artifice au réalisme: L'évolution des 'chinoiseries' théâtrales dans la première moitié du 18e siècle," *Dix-huitième siècle* 49, 1 (2017): 653–54.

15 Mathieu Deldicque, "Louis-Henri de Bourbon-Condé et la manufacture de porcelaine de Chantilly," in Mathieu Deldicque, ed., *La fabrique de l'extravagance: Porcelaines de Meissen et de Chantilly* (St-Rémy-en-l'Eau: Monelle Hayot, 2020), 54–56.

16   Antoinette Fäy-Hallé, "The Chantilly Porcelain Factory," in Pietsch and Witting, *Fascination of Fragility*, 71. Although the attempt to achieve pure, Asian-inspired "whiteness" in porcelain is generally framed as a technical quest, Chi-ming Yang has associated it with processes of racialization that emerged in the eighteenth century. See "Elephantine Chinoiserie and Asian Whiteness: Views on a Pair of Sèvres Vases," *The Journal of the Walters Art Museum* 75 (2021): https://journal.thewalters.org/2021/05/elephantine-chinoiserie-and-asian-whiteness-views-on-a-pair-of-sevres-vases/ (accessed October 10, 2021).

17   Tamara Préaud and Antoine d'Albis, *La porcelaine de Vincennes* (Paris: Adam Biro, 1991), 13–14.

18   Deldicque, "Louis-Henri de Bourbon-Condé," 55.

19   Deldicque, "Louis-Henri de Bourbon-Condé," 56; and Munger, *European Porcelain*, 52.

20   Munger, *European Porcelain*, 152.

21   Préaud and d'Albis, *La porcelaine de Vincennes*, 14.

22   Préaud and d'Albis, *La porcelaine de Vincennes*, 14.

23   Préaud and d'Albis, *La porcelaine de Vincennes*, 18.

24   Préaud and d'Albis, *La porcelaine de Vincennes*, 22.

25   Marie-Laure de Rochebrune, "L'inspiration chinoise à la manufacture royale de porcelaine de Vincennes-Sèvres," in *Pagodes et Dragons*, ed. Brunel, 113.

26   Angela Caròla-Perrotti, "Real Fabbrica di Capodimonte in Naples," in Pietsch and Witting, *Fascination of Fragility*, 89; and Munger, *European Porcelain*, 34.

27   Caròla-Perrotti, "Real Fabbrica di Capodimonte," 89.

28   Vega de Martini, "Giuseppe Gricci, c. 1700 Florence—Buen Retiro 1770," in *The Golden Age of Naples: Art and Civilization under the Bourbons, 1734–1805*, exh. cat., 2 vols. (Detroit: Detroit Institute of Arts and Chicago: The Art Institute of Chicago, 1981), 2: 385; Caròla-Perrotti, "Real Fabbrica di Capodimonte"; and Munger, *European Porcelain*, 34.

29   Caròla-Perrotti, "Real Fabbrica di Capodimonte," 89.

30   Caròla-Perrotti, "Real Fabbrica di Capodimonte," 90.

31   Elizabeth Adams, "The Chelsea Porcelain Factory," in Pietsch and Witting, *Fascination of Fragility*, 107–109; Munger, *European Porcelain*, 247.

32   Munger, *European Porcelain*, 247.

33   Adams, "The Chelsea Porcelain Factory," 107.

34   Adams, "The Chelsea Porcelain Factory," 107; and Munger, *European Porcelain*, 249.

35   Adams, "The Chelsea Porcelain Factory," 107.

36   Munger, *European Porcelain*, 253–55.

37   Hsin-yun Ou, "*The Chinese Festival* and the Eighteenth-Century London Audience," *The Wenshan Review of Literature and Culture* 2, 1 (December 2008): 31–52.

38   The exhibition *Colonial Philadelphia Porcelain: The Art of Bonnin and Morris* was presented at the Philadelphia Museum of Art from March 8–June 1, 2008. See https://www.philamuseum.org/exhibitions/261.html?page=1 (accessed October 28, 2021).

39   See the artist's interview with Marianne Brouwer, "A Zero Degree of Writing and Other Subversive Moments: An Interview with Ni Haifeng," in Roel Arkesteijn and Ni Haifeng, *Ni Haifeng: No-Man's Land* (Amsterdam: Artimo, 2003), 46–55.

II

Artistic Interventions

II

Artistic Interventions

COSTUME DESIGN

Q&A with Harriet Jung

MEREDITH MARTIN *What was your reaction when Phil first approached you about this project?*

HARRIET JUNG I was very intrigued by the premise and was excited to be given an opportunity to work solo. I usually work as part of a design duo and am rarely approached to work on something alone. It is also rare to be working on a team of mostly Asian Americans, which was appealing to me since I am usually working with teams of mostly white people.

MM *Can you talk about the research you did and how it informed your designs?*

HJ I looked through many images of porcelain from the same time period as the ballet. I was also in conversation with you about which styles were prevalent and trending during that time, particularly Kakiemon, and what the initial visual ideas might have been for the *Ballet des Porcelaines*—although we definitely took some liberties with this, for example by costuming the musicians in robes to serve as our porcelain "set" [Fig. 40]. A floral print from a Meissen teapot in the collection of the Gardiner Museum in Toronto is a main feature of the designs, for the costumes of both the Princess and the Sorcerer [Figs. 41, 43, and 44]. It is a nod to the era and Augustus the Strong's Meissen manufactory but also a reference to the ballet's other name, *The Teapot Prince*.

For the Prince's outfit and mask, I borrowed a prunus, or plum, blossom detail of a Meissen plate from the collection of The Metropolitan Museum of Art [Figs. 42, 45, and 46]. Known as *Meihua* in Chinese, these blossoms emerge in winter and, as harbingers of spring, are an auspicious symbol celebrating the renewal of life and new beginnings. The inventory mark of the plate indicates that it was owned by Augustus the Strong. The Sorcerer's mask was inspired by a pagod figurine of the same era as the ballet [Fig. 47; see also Fig. 7].

MM *What role does drawing play in your design process?*

HJ I generally spend a lot of time sketching rough ideas. Sketching helps me get thoughts down quickly and allows me to refine the idea from there. I continually edit and tweak my ideas, and therefore my sketches, sometimes even as the process of producing the garments is underway.

FIGURE 40

Harriet Jung, sketch for the musicians' robes for the *Ballet des Porcelaines*, 2021. Courtesy of the artist.

FIGURES 41–43

Harriet Jung, sketches
for the costumes of the
Princess, the Prince,
and the Sorcerer, 2021.
Courtesy of the artist.

FIGURE 44

Harriet Jung, Sorcerer's headpiece, 2021.
Courtesy of the artist.

FIGURE 45

Harriet Jung, Prince's mask, 2021.
Courtesy of the artist.

FIGURE 46

Plate with tiger and bamboo, c. 1730.
Meissen manufactory, hard-paste porcelain
painted with colored enamels over transparent
glaze, 7 × 37.8 cm. The Metropolitan Museum of
Art, The George B. McClellan Collection, Gift of
Mrs. George B. McClellan, 1941 (42.205.125).

FIGURE 47

Harriet Jung, Sorcerer's pagod mask, 2021.
Courtesy of the artist.

MM *Many ballets are about metamorphosis, but you had the unique challenge of having the characters transform and change costumes multiple times over the course of a short work. How did you handle this?*

HJ This was very restricted, due to this ballet being a small production and due to some of the transformations having to happen on "stage." As primarily a dance designer, I felt that unitards were a must as the base layer of transformation. Working closely with the choreographer, Phil Chan, allowed for these multiple transformations to fit seamlessly into the dance.

CHOREOGRAPHY

Q&A with Xin Ying

MEREDITH MARTIN What was your reaction when Phil first approached you about this project?

XIN YING I was excited because I had heard about Phil and the incredible work that he and Gina [Georgina Pazcoguin] were doing through Final Bow for Yellowface. He told me about the project and the fact that no one really knew about this historical ballet, but that instead of this being a problem, or instead of trying to bring it back to life, they were going to create a modern version with a twist on the Asian perspective. For that reason only, I was all for it; I wanted to be part of the project no matter what.

MM How is baroque ballet/movement different from the modern and contemporary dance you perform as a principal with the Martha Graham company?

XY It's very different from modern dance and especially from the Graham technique. There, you use movement to express and expose your inner emotions. With baroque ballet, I think you hide them. It is much more restrained and you can't really express your emotions much; it's just very proper and delicate and the movement is smaller. That was definitely a challenge for me. But I loved it, especially working with Patricia [Beaman]; she was such a good communicator between dance languages, and she knew how to show me a new ballet term and make me remember it. It's really not my own language at all, so it took some time,

FIGURE 48

Xin Ying dancing the Princess's saraband during rehearsal at NYU's Center for Ballet and the Arts, September 2021. Photo: Phil Chan.

but I was glad that she and Phil were so patient with me. You can experience, with baroque dance, that it's very proper and formal, and you have to pay attention to every little gesture. Be in control, don't overdo it. Sometimes that is even harder than actually expressing emotion. So that was very interesting for me.

MM What other kinds of dance, movement, and expression did you incorporate into the choreography?

XY Well, my background is Martha Graham, and of course I incorporated some of that. I also had training in Chinese classical dance when I was younger. It was really good to know that Phil was also trained in classical Chinese and to see how he incorporated that into the work—at times I was like, wow, he's bringing out the fan now, he's bringing out the sword dance, so that gave me a bit of nostalgia. And I was able to get out my fan, do a little fan dance and wrist movement [Fig. 48]. It made me feel very authentic in my own body and it felt right to be the person involved in this project. I really enjoyed my artistic process and collaboration with Phil. We have a similar training background and we have a lot in common. It felt like we were speaking the same language in an almost effortless way.

Of course, I brought contemporary and modern movement and ideas into the piece as well—for example, when the Princess encounters the Sorcerer and is controlled by his magic. I did some improvising to convey that kind of inner struggle and complex feeling at that moment. She's not just longing for her lover or looking for her lover; she has to be desirable to the Sorcerer, sexy and flirtatious but also with her dignity underneath. She has to protect herself, but she also needs to know how to save her lover, and she has to almost give up her dignity and sacrifice herself in exchange for her lover's life. So that was very complex, and what I did just felt right. I made a little improv, then we slowly put it into a denser language that is pretty modern and contemporary and really brings the emotion out, using the body instead of just doing steps that, as I said before, were very formal. This felt very real and raw.

MM Did this experience make you want to reimagine other historical works, even those that may have offensive or objectionable subject matter? If so, do you have a project in mind?

XY Yes, absolutely, one hundred percent. It made me feel the need to communicate between the present and the past and to bring a new perspective to a historical project—in part to know more about history and about how people thought back then, but also to know more about people living now. In Chinese we have a quotation from the Tang Dynasty emperor Li Shimin about using the past as a mirror to understand the present, to know more about humanity and about yourself. So I definitely want to do more of these kinds of works.

MM Do you have a project in mind?

XY Well, I'm very interested in a classic Chinese love story that we call *Liang Zhu* (*Butterfly Lovers*). It's similar to *Romeo and Juliet*, which is itself interesting—the fact that two different cultures have very similar love stories, kind of crossing in a way. I would love to make a contemporary version of that. And it was absolutely a pleasure working with Phil and with Georgina, and I hope we can do it more.

FIGURE 49

Patricia Beaman demonstrating baroque movement to Daniel Applebaum (Prince) and Tyler Hanes (Sorcerer) at NYU's Center for Ballet and the Arts, May 2021. Photo: Anna Sujin Leckie.

PATRICIA BEAMAN

ENTERING THE IVORY TOWER OF BAROQUE BALLET

Oftentimes, French baroque ballet—a jewel-like form of court dance whose origins stretch back to the seventeenth century—is merely perceived as a stepping-stone to classical ballet. Even Francine Lancelot, *grande dame* of baroque dance scholarship, once mused, "How to bring Belle Dance out of the ivory tower where very few ever come to visit?"¹ Yet baroque ballet is worthy of closer scrutiny and can tell us a great deal about French culture and history: potent political narratives were frequently transformed into metaphorical messages that were couched behind the entertaining beauty of aristocratic dance. Another aspect often passed over in examining these ballets is recognizing how and why imperialist and colonialist agendas shaped French court entertainment. As France's trade agreements and global explorations increased, a fantastical vision of Turkish, Asian, and New World cultures supplanted a long-term engagement with Greece and Rome, and these cultures were keenly interpreted and imitated in French art, literature, and ballet. The comte de Caylus's *Ballet des Porcelaines* (1739) evinces this French fixation upon other cultures, and also demonstrates the pervasive themes of domination and exoticism in court entertainment.

My own research into the relationship between colonialism and dance began in earnest when I started writing a textbook on dances outside of the Western tradition. More often than not, dance was a target that was irrevocably altered or eradicated as a result of colonial domination. I was compelled to look at my own history as a Western woman, trained in modern dance, who had enjoyed a long and meaningful career with the New York Baroque Dance Company.² I was struck as I began to realize how many baroque court entertainments had been shaped by French interests in other parts of the world. These *ballets de cour* craftily transmitted political messages lauding the superiority of French monarchs, often at the expense of other cultures. Some examples include *La Délivrance de Renaud* (1617), *Le Grand bal de la douairière de Billebahaut* (1626), *Le Bourgeois gentilhomme* (1670), and *Les Indes galantes* (1735)—royal spectacles created during the respective reigns of Louis XIII, Louis XIV, and Louis XV that manifest both wonder and derision for the unfamiliar "other." While the more diminutive *Ballet des Porcelaines* was presented at a private château, its themes of porcelain, power, and manipulation reflect the same obsession with other cultures—in this case, China.

Meredith Martin is not a choreographer or a dancer, but rather an art historian who specializes in examining early modern interactions with Asia in French art. It is unusual and exciting to me that a professional in another discipline would endeavor to reimagine this petite ballet. But in the current climate, sensitivity in the presentation of other cultures has rightly become a major concern. The *Ballet des Porcelaines*, also called *The Teapot Prince*, could easily be dismissed by today's standards as an Orientalist pursuit. To this end, Meredith engaged the choreographer

Phil Chan and a stellar cast of Asian and Asian American dancers, designers, and musicians in order to embrace the "with us, not without us" ethic that has become so imperative to address. The fact that this ballet apparently had not been restaged since 1741 was freeing in that there was no precedent—no lingering memory of what came before. Meredith and Phil chose not to adhere to a strict historical restaging, yet in the interest of honoring the cultural specificity of the dance, they asked if I could lend a hand by consulting on baroque movement and gesture. Deep into the pandemic on one cold, bright winter day, Phil and I met by the carousel in Brooklyn Bridge Park. With notation in hand, I taught him the man's part of *Sarabande d'Issé*, a beautiful and complex dance that he picked up remarkably quickly.[3] Dancing that duet was the beginning of our journey into the eighteenth century.

Baroque dance is like a porcelain figure—small, delicate, and with great attention to detail: a rotation of the lower leg, a turn of the hand, a curve of the arm are all executed in a much subtler manner than in classical ballet. Because of the lack of high extensions and pyrotechnical virtuosity, the understated quality of baroque technique is often perceived as being less difficult than ballet and contemporary dance, yet the specificity and precision that underlie all solid technique is absolutely inherent in this form as well. I wasn't sure how my efforts would be received by the dancers, but they were all consummate professionals who were open to and truly curious about being brought back in time (Fig. 49). The biggest challenges were dialing down many basic movements that any contemporary or ballet dancer develops in their practice. For instance, the baroque version of the *port de bras* (carriage of the arms) is extremely rounded and held low, while today's dancers are used to the arms veering toward greater extension (Fig. 50). The height of the legs—a major feature of both classical ballet and many forms of modern and contemporary dance—also had to be brought down to forty-five degrees in keeping with the style. In his embrace of the spirit of the eighteenth century, Phil's choreography has been infused with much of the flavor, nuance, and grace of baroque dance. In Martin and Chan's distinctive, reimagined production of the *Ballet des Porcelaines*, the ivory tower has been visited. I'm honored to have been of help.

[1]   Francine Lancelot, *La Belle Danse* (Paris: Van Dieren
Éditeur, 1996), xi (translation mine).

[2]   NYBDC was founded in 1976 by Catherine Turocy,
Artistic Director, and Ann Jacoby.

[3]   From the opera *Issé* by composer André Cardinal
Destouches (1697); Feuillet notation of the
choreography by Anthony L'Abbé is found
in L'Abbé's *A New Collection of Dances* (London:
F. Le Rousseau, c. 1725).

LEAH GALE NELSON

MUSICALLY STEEPING A POT OF TEA

When our colleague Patricia Beaman introduced us to Meredith Martin and this project, Dongsok Shin and I were intrigued by her ideas and by this action-packed, informative little manuscript. Mid-pandemic we were happy to grant Meredith and Phil Chan's wish for a general sense of the score, with Dongsok recording the music on harpsichord. From there, Phil launched his remarkable choreographic vision, infused with baroque elements, connecting the eras through his artistry.

Combining historical performance practices with modern performance creates a bridge for today's audience to connect with the past while experiencing

QUATRIEME CHAMBRE DES APARTEMENS.

something new, together evoking timeless emotions of joy, fear, sorrow, and triumph. It is a passion we share, keeping a repertoire alive that would otherwise be misunderstood or lost, bringing it to life in a way that entertains and speaks to us today. With the *Ballet des Porcelaines* project, we share in the opportunity to present a part of history musically, while bringing the subjects into fresh relief for our own time, further opening our eyes culturally to the subjects in both contexts—then, and now.

Having an understanding of the performance practices, musical instruments, and dance of eighteenth-century France gives us the ability to speak the language of the music on the page. As Patricia describes in her essay for this volume, the subtleties, specificity, and precision in baroque dance, the players likewise immersed in detail, render what looks to be a simple line of music into something exquisite, evocative, and moving to the ear and to the soul.

The musical language of 1730s France is a very specific art, steeped in traditions and standards established decades earlier by Jean-Baptiste Lully, master of music to Louis XIV, emulated throughout Europe and a mainstay well beyond the *grande siècle*. As baroque performers and confessed Francophiles, we have explored the *musique de la chambre* of Louis XIV and beyond (Fig. 51). The ongoing tradition of weekly entertainments, for *Concerts Royeaux* and *Appartements*, etc., included suites of dances for small instrumental ensembles and cantatas (essentially miniature operas for the living room) where a singer or two joins in. Volumes of this popular genre were filled with epic tales—*Orphée*, *Médée*, *La Mort de Didon*, etc.—where singers narrate the stories while instruments enhance and reinforce the narratives, combining text and music to guide the drama.

In a pantomime (*ballet en action*), the instruments become the narrators, as in our *Teapot Prince*, with the "text" articulated through the instrumental writing. From the fleeing of the prince, to the immense presence of the sorcerer and the sorrowful princess, to the manipulation of the sorcerer, the reuniting of lovers in happiness and in tender love, to a fanfare heralding triumph—these ever-changing affects rendered by the instruments are critical to the action, and dictate the tale.

The manuscript score gives us copious, clear, ever-shifting affects—from *Vif* to *Gravement* to *Lentement*, etc.—and includes detailed stage directions (see Fig. 57). Further, the manuscript libretto includes instructions to the composer for each scene (see, for example, Fig. 54).[1] As per instruction, the instrumental narrative gives us many "quick but sustained flourishes" for the dramatic storytelling, along with a handful of proper dance forms—*sarabande*, *gigue* or *passepied*, *vaudeville*, a *contradanse*, and two *marches*. These two marches, "*airs pour les porcelaines*," strike us. In the first (Act I, Scene I), the librettist asks for sounds of porcelain gently clinking. How does one do this, with two violins and bass? The composer's answer is a march, typically a somewhat militant and brilliant form, but here sounding a little like glass, with the two violins clinking and plinking in a high register, and at moments tumbling. The march comes back to close Act II, with a quicker tempo and the instruction to be "played in full with its refrains," which the composer indulges (see Fig. 58). However, the request for music like "a sort of canary" (a fast gigue-like dance), was either disregarded or the team decided to reprise the earlier march, perhaps just with a canary effect (i.e., fleet), as this is still a march, only faster and with a second *couplet* (or instrumental verse).

[1] For the quotations from the libretto that follow, see the transcription of the original French as well as the English translation by Christine Jones in this volume.

FIGURE 52

Leah Gale Nelson performing the *Ballet des Porcelaines* at The Metropolitan Museum of Art, December 6, 2021. Photo by Jacob Blickenstaff.

The score calls for an "*ensemble en trio*"—two treble instruments, in this case violins, with *basso continuo*, which is the bass line "realized" by a team of players: for us, harpsichord, viola da gamba, and theorbo. We thought about adding continuous harmony to the violin line, since much of the writing is in unison. Instead, we chose to follow the manuscript and French traditional practice, with the violins dividing into harmony only where indicated.

We are using instruments from the era in historical setup, with bows made from patterns of late seventeenth- to early eighteenth-century models, giving us the musical tools to re-create the sounds and articulations of the time. For the premiere performance in New York's Metropolitan Museum of Art (Fig. 52), the museum kindly allowed the use of their French eighteenth-century-style, double-manual harpsichord, made by William Hyman, pitched at a'=392 Hz, which accurately reflects historical models. It is perfect for this pot of tea.

FINDING THE SOUND IN BETWEEN

As a second-generation Filipinx American, cobbled and lost histories, colonialism, and ambiguous bloodlines are parts of my identity. As a composer with a background in classical piano, my approach to music involves the tension of working within the context of Western music and pushing against it as best I can—for example, via deconstruction or bastardized techniques.

When Phil Chan approached me about writing interludes for *Ballet des Porcelaines*, I was 1) thrilled to work with Phil on music for dance, and 2) nervous about how my music would fit into a reimagined baroque opera where the Asian references are clearly East Asian, and more specifically, Chinese.

It was determined at the beginning that broken porcelain sounds would be part of the musical interludes. For the rest of the score, I asked myself questions: How do I create something that serves the goal of the work while making sure my own voice comes through? Am I going to be asked to reference Chinese folk tunes, and if so, is that appropriate coming from me? Or is it appropriation?

An open-minded and encouraging collaborator, Phil reminded me that he wanted to work with me for me, and wanted what I had to offer. Phil cleverly dubbed the interludes "kintsugi" music at an early point in the process, making it clear that he was down with mixing things up: accuracy of tradition was not sacred or precious in *Porcelaines*. (*Kintsugi* is a Japanese art form where broken pottery is mended with liquid gold, silver, or platinum, turning a damaged item into something beautiful, even cherished.)

I decided to dig into the artifice of ballet: no traditional instruments, or any acoustic instruments at all, only samples of them. Even vocal lines would be samples. To create a sense of cohesiveness with the baroque score, I manipulated demo recordings of the ballet (created by Dongsok Shin and Leah Gale Nelson for rehearsals) in different ways—reversing, adding effects, decreasing tempo, etc.—using the prerecorded audio as a sort of blending tool for my *kintsugi* music. I scored the music to the dancers' rehearsal videos, which were enormously helpful in regard to pacing and marking significant moments through sound.

My favorite part of the process was breaking porcelain with a hammer at the studio of the band San Fermin! Many thanks to Allen Tate for hooking that up.

III

The Lost Ballet

III

The Lost Ballet

THE MANUSCRIPT

Libretto and Score

Second Acte.

P.re Scene

La Princesse Seule.

Elle arrive en dansant et en exprimant [sa] tristesse et Son inquiétude elle cherch[e] Son Amant dans un Séjour qui lui est inc[...] et ou elle a été attirée malgré elle

Musique.

Cette danse en une espece de Sarabande tendre, languissante, plaintive, elle doi[t] auoir environ 20 mesures on pourroit [...] donner le Caractere d'un Monologu[e] D'Opera en rondeau, Le Spectateur p[ar] habitude y mettra par Sentiment des par[...] convenables.

Le Prince Pot a Thé.

Ballet pantomine.

Acte 1.er

Scene p.re.

On voit paroître dans châque aile du Théatre un Danseur ou une Danseuse, changés en Vases de Porcelaine, ensorte que çette nouveauté, fait une sorte de changement de décoration et prépare çe qui doit arriuer. afin qu'on ne doute pas que çe Soient des Acteurs, il faut que Sur une douzaine de mesures, ceux qui Sortiront des Coulisses a droite traversent le Théatre S'en [...]

FIGURES 53–54

Le Prince Pot-à-Thé (The Teapot Prince) libretto, 1739: Act I, Scene I; Act II, Scene I, "The Princess Alone". Bibliothèque nationale de France, Arts du spectacle, MY 354. Photos by Geoffrey Ripert.

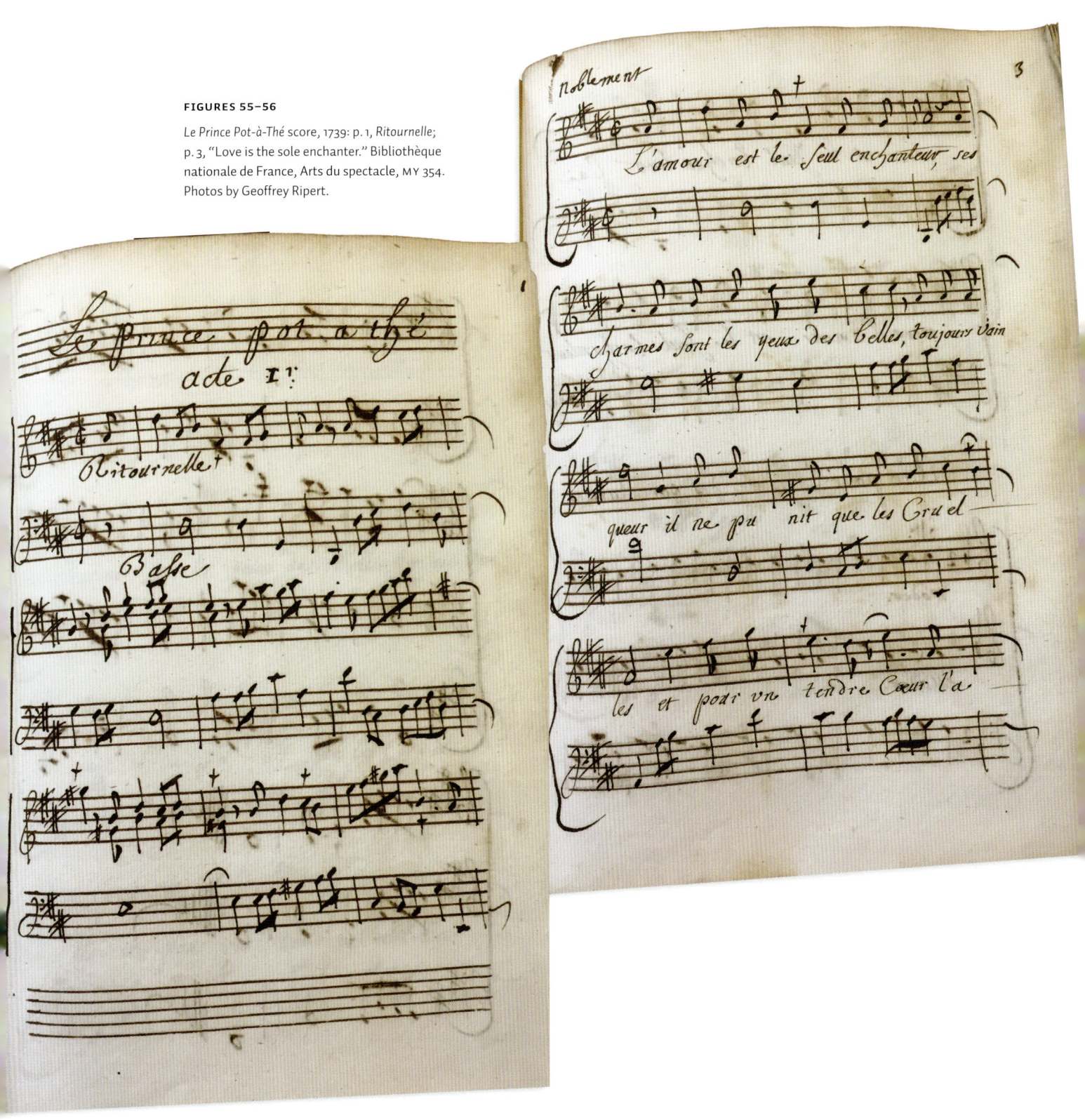

FIGURES 55–56

Le Prince Pot-à-Thé score, 1739: p. 1, *Ritournelle*; p. 3, "Love is the sole enchanter." Bibliothèque nationale de France, Arts du spectacle, MY 354. Photos by Geoffrey Ripert.

FIGURES 57–58

Le Prince Pot-à-Thé score, 1739: p. 9, "The Prince wants to evade the Sorcerer"; p. 20, Air pour les porcelaines. Bibliothèque nationale de France, Arts du spectacle, MY 354. Photos by Geoffrey Ripert.

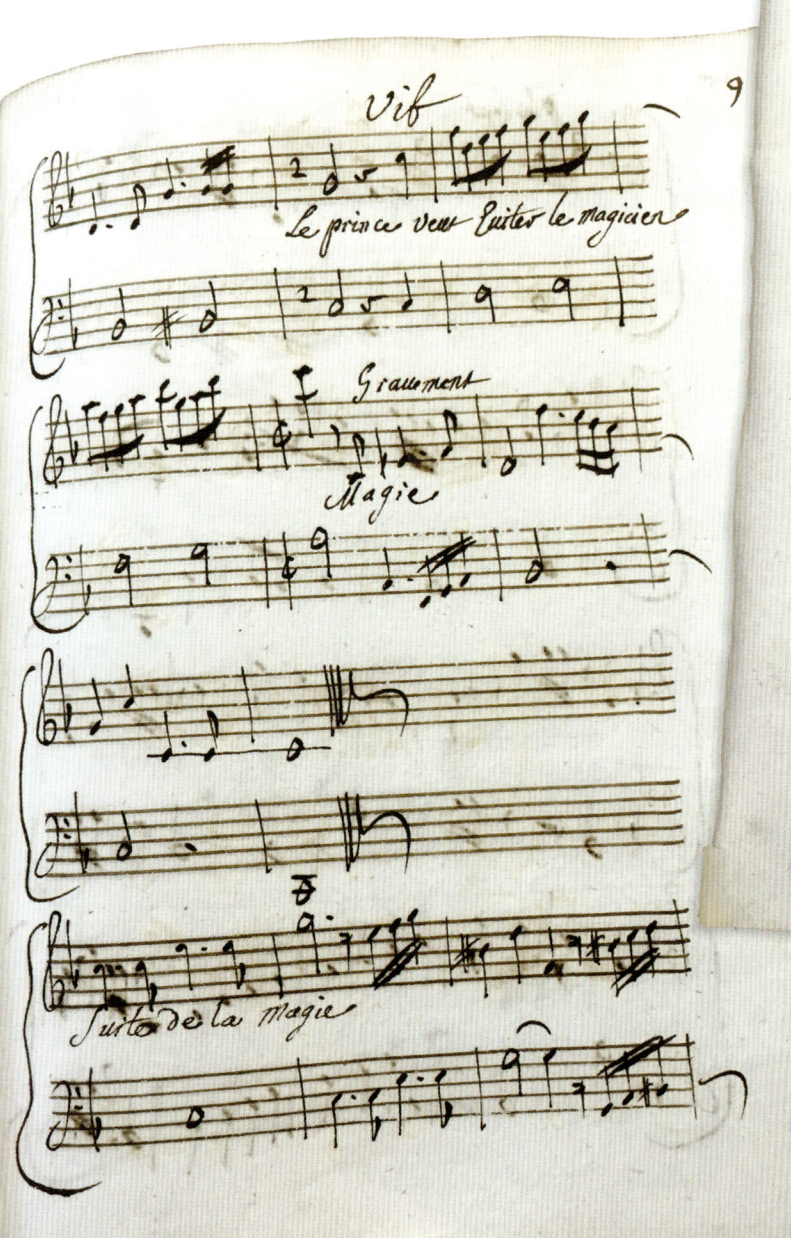

LE PRINCE POT-À-THÉ : BALLET PANTOMIME

French Transcription

ACTE Ier

Ritournelle[1]

L'amour est le seul enchanteur,   noblement
Ses charmes sont les yeux des belles,
Toujours vainqueur
Il ne punit que les cruelles
Et pour un tendre cœur
L'amour est le seul enchanteur
L'amour, l'amour est le seul enchanteur.

SCÈNE PREMIÈRE

On voit paraître dans chaque aile du théâtre un danseur ou une danseuse changés en vases [*sic*] de Porcelaine, en sorte que cette nouveauté fait une sorte de changement de décoration et prépare ce qui doit arriver afin qu'on ne doute pas que ce soient des acteurs. Il faut que sur une douzaine de mesures, ceux qui sortiront des coulisses à droite traversent le théâtre en marchant lentement et en clopinant pour venir se placer dans les ailes de la gauche et réciproquement ceux de la gauche à la droite.

La facilité de cette marche permet de déguiser en porcelaine, non seulement les acteurs qui sauront danser, mais les valets de la maison, pour garnir et décorer les deux côtés en le fond du théâtre.

D'ailleurs, il suffira pour les valets de porter un grand carton découpé, et comme ils ne feront jamais que traverser une ou plusieurs fois au gré du maître de ballet, il ne leur faudra point comme aux danseurs et danseuses un habit de porcelaine de ronde bosse.

MUSIQUE

Air pour l'arrivée des porcelaines

Il faut pour l'article précédent environ 15 ou 20 mesures de marche à notes égales en trio, c'est-à-dire que les violons jouent par accord le 1er et le second dessus et non pas à partie séparée. Il faut que cela imite en quelque façon le bruit que des porcelaines feraient en se choquant légèrement.

THE TEAPOT PRINCE: A PANTOMIME BALLET

Annotated English Translation

ACT I

Ritornello[1]

Love is the sole enchanter,   (nobly)
The eyes of beauties are his jewels,
Always the victor
He punishes the cruel
And for a heart so tender
Love is the sole enchanter
Love, love is the sole enchanter.

SCENE 1

Male or female dancers transformed into porcelain vases[2] appear on each side of the theater. The novelty of their costumes creates a change of scenery and prepares [the audience for] what is about to happen. So that there is no doubt these are actors, for a dozen measures, those that emerge from the wings on the right cross the theater ambling slowly and position themselves on the left; those on the left cross to the right.[3]

Because the procession is simple, the servants[4] as well as the actor-dancers can be costumed as porcelain to adorn and decorate both sides of the theater and upstage.

In fact, the servants can simply wear a large decoupage,[5] as they will only cross the theater once or twice, at the Ballet Master's discretion; they certainly do not need to wear the dimensional porcelain costume that the male and female dancers wear.[6]

MUSIC

Melody for the Entry of the Porcelain

The above procession calls for about 15 to 20 measures of a march played with equal notes and en trio; that is to say, the first and second treble violins play in unison and not as separate parts.[7] It should sound a bit like the noise porcelain makes if you clink pieces together gently.

SCÈNE 2ᵉ

Les Porcelaines étant rangées

Fuite du prince.   *vif*
Surprise et étonnement du prince.   *Lentement*

On voit paraître le Prince ou le Berger, car l'habit qu'on se trouvera décidera de sa condition. Il exprime par ses pas et ses attitudes, qu'il fuit un péril prochain, et il marque aussi son étonnement de se trouver dans un lieu aussi singulier, où il ne voit que des Porcelaines, car le spectacle serait complet s'il y en avait de peintes dans la décoration.

MUSIQUE

20 mesures de musique vive qui commence par exprimer la fuite, et qui par des traits de chants rapides mais suspendus, exprime la surprise et l'étonnement.

SCÈNE 3ᵉ

Magie.   *gravement*
Le prince veut éviter le magicien.   *vif*
Magie.   *gravement*
Suite de la magie.
Le prince et le magicien paraissent.
Joie du magicien.

Le Magicien arrive. Il poursuit le Prince qui tâche à s'éloigner de lui, mais qui paraît retenu par le pouvoir des enchantements et des cercles et autres figures magiques que fait autour de lui le Magicien. Enfin le Magicien le touche de sa baguette. Le Prince fait quelques pas chancelants en s'éloignant vers la coulisse et le Magicien le suit, tenant toujours sa baguette sur le Prince et faisant des pas graves et terribles. Ils disparaissent tous deux. La symphonie poursuit quelques mesures, et l'on voit rentrer avec les mêmes pas lents le Prince changé en porcelaine et le Magicien qui le suit pas à pas en tenant toujours sa baguette sur la porcelaine dans la même attitude où il la tenait sur le Prince, qui s'arrête au milieu du fond du théâtre où il reste immobile. Le Magicien, après quelques mesures qu'il danse seul, se retire.

MUSIQUE

Le magicien arrive. Musique magique de six mesures.
Le Prince tourne autour de lui en cherchant à l'éviter. Musique rapide 2 ou 3 mesures.
Le magicien fait des cercles. Musique magique 2 ou trois mesures.
[Le magicien touche le prince avec sa baguette. Musique magique, qui devient plus lente à mesure que le Prince s'affaiblit et qu'ils se cachent tous deux dans la coulisse. Elle continue dans le même caractère de lenteur jusqu'à ce qu'ils rentrent tous deux et que le prince, changé en porcelaine, soit au milieu du théâtre, où il reste immobile. 30 mesures.]

SCENE 2

The Porcelain Arranged

Prince's escape   (*lively*)
Prince's surprise and shock   (*slow*)

The Prince or Shepherd (depending on the costume available[8]) arrives. In his steps and body language, he expresses that he is fleeing impending danger and registers surprise at finding himself in such a curious place, where he sees only porcelain; indeed, the spectacle would be complete if there were also painted objects in the [stage] decoration.[9]

MUSIC

20 lively measures that begin by expressing flight and then, with quick but sustained flourishes, express wonder and surprise.

SCENE 3

Magic   (*somber*)
Prince wants to evade Sorcerer   (*lively*)
Magic   (*somber*)
Magic continues   (*slower*)
Prince and Sorcerer enter
Sorcerer's delight[10]

The Sorcerer enters in pursuit of the Prince, who attempts to get away from him but is visibly held back by the power of the spells, circles, and other ritual movements that the Sorcerer makes around him. Finally, the Sorcerer taps him with his magic wand. The Prince stumbles towards the wings and the Sorcerer follows in a slow, menacing gait, his wand still pointing at the Prince. They both disappear offstage. The music continues for a few measures and then the Prince, transformed into porcelain, and the Sorcerer come back onstage in the same slow gait. The Sorcerer follows right behind the porcelain, still pointing his wand at it the way he pointed it at the Prince. The porcelain Prince stops upstage center and stands still. After dancing on his own for a few measures, the Sorcerer exits.

MUSIC

{The Sorcerer enters. Magical music for 6 measures.
{The Prince darts around him, trying to avoid him. Quick music for 2 or 3 measures.
{The Sorcerer makes circles [with his wand]. Magical music for 2 or 3 measures.
({30 measures: the Sorcerer taps the Prince with his wand. Magical music that slows as the Prince weakens and they exit into the wings. The music continues in the same slow vein until they both reenter and the Prince, transformed into porcelain, is in the middle of the stage, where he stands still.)[11]

Le magicien le quitte, et danse seul. Musique plus vive et qui exprime la joie du Magicien,
qui sort après avoir dansé, environ 10 mesures.
La symphonie reprend les 10 dernières mesures après que le magicien est sorti, ce qui sert
d'entre acte.

SECOND ACTE

SCÈNE PREMIÈRE

La Princesse seule

Elle arrive en dansant et en exprimant sa tristesse et son inquiétude ; elle cherche
son amant dans un séjour qui lui est inconnu et où elle a été attirée malgré elle.

MUSIQUE

Sarabande.
Tristesse et inquiétude de la princesse.

Cette danse est une espèce de sarabande tendre, languissante, plaintive. Elle doit avoir environ
20 mesures. On pourrait lui donner le caractère d'un monologue d'opéra en rondeau. Le spectateur
par habitude y mettra par sentiment des paroles convenables.

SCÈNE 2ᵉ

Le Magicien, La Princesse

Effroi de la Princesse à l'arrivée du Magicien.
Il se présente à elle d'un air soumis.   *posément*
Elle veut le fuir.
Il l'arrête.   *fièrement*
Elle feint de l'écouter.   *un peu doux*
Il se jette à ses pieds.
Elle le flatte.   *tendrement et un peu doux*
Il témoigne sa joie.   *fort*
Elle continue la feinte et l'engage à la laisser seule.   *tendrement et doux*
Il sort.

MUSIQUE

En dialoguant cette scène on ne peut pas manquer de la bien faire.
Elle ne doit pas avoir plus de 30 mesures.

{The Sorcerer leaves him and dances alone. Livelier music now expresses the Sorcerer's delight. He exits after dancing about 10 measures.
{Once the Sorcerer has exited, the musicians repeat the last 10 measures, which serve as an intermission.

ACT II

SCENE 1

The Princess Alone

She dances onstage expressing sadness and apprehension. She is searching for her lover in a place she does not know and that she was drawn to in spite of herself.

MUSIC

Sarabande
Princess's Sadness and Apprehension

She dances an emotional, languid, and plaintive Sarabande for about 20 measures.[12] It can have the feel of an opera Rondeau monologue.[13] A seasoned audience will know the appropriate words to put to it.

SCENE 2

The Sorcerer, The Princess

Princess's terror at the Sorcerer's entrance
He presents himself like a suitor   (*steady*)
She wants to flee
He stops her   (*arrogant*)
She pretends to listen to him   (*a little soft*)
He prostrates himself before her
She cajoles him with flattery   (*with feeling and a little soft*)
He expresses delight   (*loud*)
She continues to flatter him and manages to convince him to leave
her there alone   (*with feeling and soft*)
He exits

MUSIC

Performed as a [pantomime] dialogue, this scene always plays well.
It should last no more than 30 measures.

SCÈNE 3ᵉ

La Princesse seule

Douleur. *lentement*
Fureur.
Joie d'avoir trouvé la baguette du magicien. *gai*
Elle retombe dans l'inquiétude. *lentement*

La Princesse exprime dans ce monologue les passages de la douleur à la frayeur. Elle trouve la baguette du Magicien qu'il avait laissée à ses pieds en s'y jetant, et en lui prenant la main pour la baiser. Elle s'en saisit. Elle exprime sa joie, et retombe dans l'inquiétude. Une sorte d'inspiration la fait courir autour de toutes les Porcelaines pour chercher son amant.

MUSIQUE

Elle court autour des porcelaines pour chercher son amant. *vif*
Air pour les porcelaines. *allegro rondeau*

Tous ces différents mouvements de l'âme doivent être fort courts, et il suffit de se les peindre pour les rendre en 12 ou 15 mesures au plus.

Lorsque la Princesse parcourt le théâtre sur un air léger et agréable, toutes les porcelaines se mettent en mouvement et traversent le théâtre en différents sens et disparaissent dans les coulisses. Pendant ce temps la Princesse s'est attachée à suivre le Prince métamorphosé et elle le suit dans la coulisse, tenant toujours la baguette sur lui.

MUSIQUE

Cet air est une espèce de canarie qui imite dans un mouvement léger le choc des porcelaines. Il continue lorsque toutes les porcelaines sont hors du théâtre, et l'on entend vers la fin de l'air le bruit de toutes les porcelaines qui se cassent. Cet air est un air entier avec ses reprises. Le Maître du Ballet jugera de ce qu'il doit en faire danser et de ce qui s'en jouera pendant le vide du théâtre, pour avoir le temps d'ôter les cartons dont les acteurs seront chargés.

ACTE 3ᵉᵐᵉ

SCÈNE 1ᵉʳᵉ

Le prince et la princesse reviennent ensemble.
gai – tendrement et doux – gai et fort –
tendrement et doux –
gai et fort

SCENE 3

The Princess Alone

Pain   *(slowly)*
Rage
Delight at finding the Sorcerer's wand   *(joyous)*
She is again apprehensive   *(slowly)*

In this solo, the Princess expresses a mood swing, from pain to fury.[14] She finds the wand the Sorcerer left at her feet when he prostrated himself before her and took her hand to kiss it. She grabs it excitedly, then her apprehension returns. Some sort of force compels her to search for her lover among all the porcelain.

MUSIC

{She runs among the porcelain to find her lover.   *(lively)*
{Melody for the porcelain.   *(quick and vivacious)*[15]

These movements of the soul should be very brief and it's enough to depict them over 12 to 15 measures at most.

While the Princess makes her way across the theater to a playful and pleasing melody, all the porcelain begins to move and cross the theater on different paths before disappearing into the wings. In the meantime, the Princess has tracked the transformed Prince and follows him into the wings, her wand still pointed at him.

MUSIC

This melody is a sort of a canary jig that sounds like the light clink of porcelain against porcelain.[16] It continues until all the porcelain has left the theater and ends with the sound of all the porcelain breaking. This melody is played in full with its refrains. The Ballet Master will decide how they will dance and what to play while the theater is empty, to give the actors time to remove the decoupage.

ACT III

SCENE 1

The Prince and the Princess reenter together.
*(joyous — tender and soft — joyous and strong —
tender and soft — joyous and strong)*

IV

Contemporary Restagings

IV Contemporary Restagings

WOLF BURCHARD *The Metropolitan Museum of Art, New York*

MAKING THE PORCELAIN DANCE

One of the principal objectives of today's museum curators is to breathe life into the collections under their care and to help them tell their stories. Some objects were once personal belongings to whom a single individual developed a close emotional attachment. Others were witnesses to, or direct products of, some of the most significant chapters in the history of civilization, and most of them have multiple biographies and several stories to tell. "We have one life, they have many lives," to use Neil MacGregor's words.

The poster child of The Metropolitan Museum of Art's first-ever exhibition devoted to Walt Disney and the hand-drawn animation of his studios is a Sèvres pink porcelain tower vase, of which the fantastical architecture foreshadows Disneyland's Sleeping Beauty Castle by almost two centuries (Fig. 59). What may at first appear an odd choice illustrates the dialogue the exhibition seeks to encourage between the rhetoric, wit, and beauty of twentieth-century animated films and that of rococo decorative arts.

Only two pairs of the peculiar yet highly sophisticated tower vases were produced: a pink pair, now in the collection of the Huntington Art Museum in Pasadena, and a green one, in The Met's collection. Made around 1762–63, the four vases are being reunited in the exhibition, probably for the first time in 250 years. To this day, there remain some gaps in their respective provenance. If only these objects could speak! What would they say? And what would they say to each other? "Fancy seeing you here!" "Where were you during the French Revolution?" "When did you come to America?" It is conceivable that the vases last saw each other at Versailles in April 1763, during one of the regular sales organized by Sèvres and

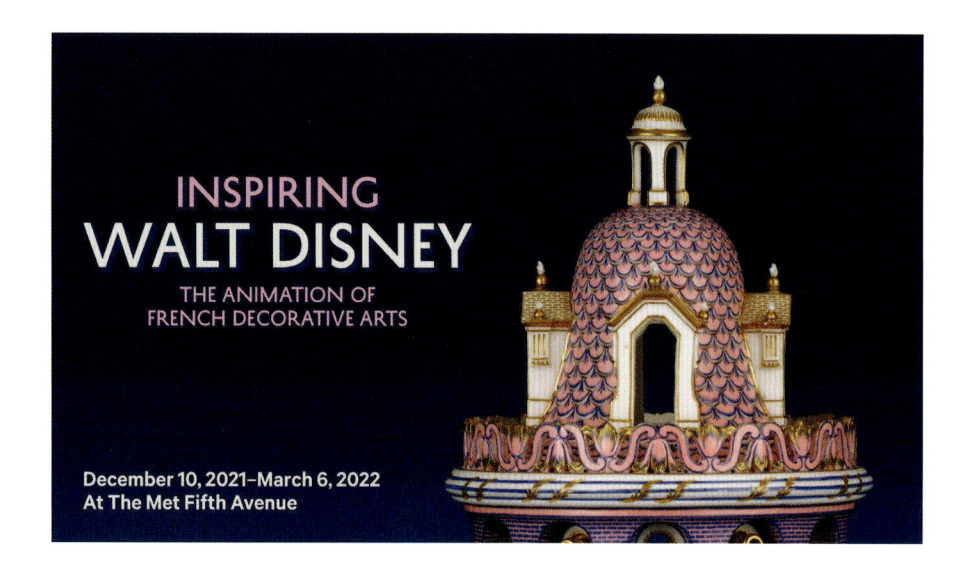

FIGURE 59

Abby Chen, Exhibition poster for *Inspiring Walt Disney* at The Metropolitan Museum of Art, 2021. Image courtesy of The Metropolitan Museum of Art.

FIGURE 60

The Magic Lantern, c. 1760. After a model by
Etienne-Maurice Falconet, Sèvres manufactory,
soft-paste biscuit porcelain, 15.6 × 17.1 × 13.3 cm.
The Metropolitan Museum of Art, Bequest of
Ella Morris de Peyster, 1957 (58.60.10).

usually attended by the French king himself. Because we tend to associate provenance with grand surnames and distinguished collections, one is compelled to
imagine a rather snooty exchange between the vases—not helped by the fact that
the pink pair was sold on the spot, while the green vases remained in the manufactory's inventory of unsold stock for at least another decade.

The tower vases are thought to have been designed by Étienne-Maurice Falconet, the French sculptor and royal academician widely known for his *Menacing
Cupid* (1757)—a work that quite literally seems to whisper to us—as well as *Pygmalion and Galatea* (1763), based on the myth of a statue animated by love that was
often performed on the eighteenth-century French stage. Appointed director of
sculpture at Sèvres in 1757, many of Falconet's marble creations were translated
into the then new medium of soft-paste biscuit porcelain. *The Magic Lantern* (c. 1760;
Fig. 60) is the first such object from The Met's collection that visitors will clap eyes
on when touring the Disney exhibition. It was part of a series of so-called Boucher

and Falconet children made at Vincennes and Sèvres, of which some of the earliest examples were supplied to Louis XV with the aim of enlivening the king's table with charmingly sentimental conversation pieces.

Depicting a novel technological device that prefigured cartoons and cinema, *The Magic Lantern* also captures the childlike wonder of storytelling upon which Disney's empire was built. Falconet's gentle rendering of the youthful spectators conveys their focused awe as well as their willingness to block out their surroundings and let their imaginations run free—one of the main themes of The Met's exhibition. That children perceived the world differently from adults was a subject of great fascination among mid-eighteenth-century French philosophers like Rousseau and Voltaire, who took a keen interest in the psychological differences between childhood and adulthood and concluded that children were not just miniature versions of adults.

This is not to say, however, that adults could not experience a similar sense of wonder, particularly in the face of new technical and artistic marvels. *The Teapot Prince*, also known as the *Ballet des Porcelaines* (1739), illustrates the allure that the magical medium of porcelain held for Voltaire's peers, the comte de Caylus, and his friends. Connecting the visual with the performing arts, the pantomime ballet conveys a key aspect of rococo culture, as it sits at the very intersection of music, dance, porcelain, and the literature of transformation made popular in the 1740s. *The Sofa: A Moral Tale* (1742), written by Caylus's friend Claude Prosper Jolyot de Crébillon, was the most widely distributed example of that genre and went through eighteen editions in London alone. It recounts the fate of Amanzéi, an Indian Brahmin, who saw his questionable behavior punished when his soul was separated from his body and sentenced to journey from one sofa to another, until he witnessed a genuine declaration of love. The colorful activities Amanzéi observed while transformed into an array of upholstered furniture were quickly recognized as thinly veiled satire of the goings-on at the court of Louis XV, leading to Crébillon's banishment from Paris for three months.

What might explain the enormous appeal of stories as well as ballets and theatrical productions told from the perspective of man-made objects? Is it that the fantasy of transformation—paramount to the success of fairy tales—allows readers to imagine that they can be whatever they want to be? Is it the draw of voyeurism, personified here by mute witnesses (like a sofa) who can relay events no other human saw? Or, finally, is it simply the widespread inclination to attribute human properties to non-living entities, i.e., anthropomorphism as a psychological and philosophical phenomenon? Humans need connection with other humans, and in the absence of other humans, they are likely to satisfy that need by anthropomorphizing other things that surround them, like pets or porcelain wares.

Anthropomorphisms are also commonplace in most religions: almost all deities of ancient Greece and Rome originated from a desire to explain natural phenomena for which there was no explanation. Not knowing where thunder and earthquakes came from, the ancients invented gods with human features who were responsible for them. In June 1765, Caylus, a mere three months before he died, presented the royal library in Paris with a small portrait of François I that ranks amongst the most eccentric likenesses of any king of France (Fig. 61). It shows the sixteenth-century sovereign in the combined guise of five Roman divinities: Mars, Minerva,

Mercury, Amor, and Diana. This visual panegyric, once attributed to Niccolò dell'Abbate, sought to make visible François's diverse qualities and virtues; "[France] . . . your great king who surpasses nature," reads the inscription below. The layering of mythological imagery, the "transformed" appearance of the Renaissance prince, and the Mannerist flamboyance of the composition are likely to have appealed to the antiquarian mind of Caylus, who also viewed this small wooden panel as a "speaking" bystander of history, according to the note he attached to the back of it, indicating that it was drawn from life and thus witnessed the presence of the king it depicts.

Figurative representations accompanied by detailed captions are, of course, more likely to speak to us directly than decorative objects that require additional assistance to have their stories told. The intricate iconography of a Renaissance portrait such as that of François I addresses our intellect, while rococo decorative arts call upon our senses. Indeed, the very power of the latter objects lies in their being emotional works of art that prompt a visceral rather than a cerebral response. The same is true of Disney hand-drawn animated films. Walt Disney famously said, "I make pictures for entertainment, and then the professors tell me what they mean." Would the Sèvres craftspeople express similar sentiments, when confronted with recent interpretations of their works?

On can but speculate about their artistic motivations, for like their ceramics, these makers remain predominately silent, having left no records akin to the lively debates held at the French royal academies of painting, sculpture, and architecture. As Katie Scott explains, "if there was no textual defence of decoration in the eighteenth century it is precisely because its authors belonged, in a very real sense, to the non-literate world of work."[1] I would argue that objects such as the tower vases were made with one very simple goal: giving their audience pleasure; maybe helping them escape, albeit for a brief moment, the tribulation of ordinary life through magic, beguilement, sometimes even contemplation. That is certainly what *The Teapot Prince* does, but more importantly, Caylus's ballet, in its ambitions, reveals itself as a manifestation of what museums should aspire to: bringing their objects to life. The Met looks back at a long tradition devoted to this quest. Famously, upon his appointment as the museum's new director in 1967, Thomas Hoving received the brief from New York's then-mayor John V. Lindsay to "make the mummies dance." Half a century later, it may be the turn of the porcelain.

FIGURE 61

Master of the Hours of Henri II, *François Ier as a Composite Deity*, c. 1545. Gouache on parchment pasted on an oak panel, 23.4 × 13.4 cm. Bibliothèque Nationale de France, Paris. © Gallica BnF.

---

1   Katie Scott, "Hierarchy, Liberty and Order: Languages of Art and Institutional Conflict in Paris (1766–1776)," *Oxford Art Journal* 12, 2 (1989): 59.

JUDITH T. ZEITLIN *The University of Chicago*

CHINESE FANTASIES OF PORCELAIN

On the Cusp Between Life and Death

Sometime between 1433, when the eunuch admiral Zheng He made his final maritime expedition to the Indian Ocean and South China Sea, and 1522, an anonymous opera script celebrating his exploits entitled *Voyage to the Western Ocean* was deposited in the Ming palace theater bureau.[1] We don't know if this opera was ever actually performed, though there is no reason it would not have been. Liana Chen rightly sees it as a precursor of the "tribute paying" theatricals performed on diplomatic and ceremonial occasions at the Qing court, the kind prepared for Lord Macartney in 1793 during his diplomatic mission from Great Britain to China.[2] Such spectacular pageants typically included scenes of foreign envoys flocking to the Chinese court to present accolades and rare treasures as an act of submission to the ruling dynasty and its cultural and moral superiority. They were not so unlike the *ballet des nations* genre popular at the seventeenth- and eighteenth-century French court, which featured performers exotically costumed as princes from around the world, including China, extolling the virtues and beauties of France.[3]

In one interlude in *Voyage to the Western Ocean*, "barbarian" rulers of three island kingdoms (Sulu in the Philippines, Pahang in Malaysia, and a mythical "Land of Pierced Hearts"), desperate to hijack the precious cargo of the admiral's fleet of "treasure boats," convene on an "Island of Disorderly Rocks" to blockade his ships as a way of extorting what they most desire: porcelain.[4] As a sign, perhaps, of their rustic boorishness in Ming Chinese eyes, it's not the beauty of porcelain dishes that they prize, but the material's utilitarian ability to hold hot and cold substances without cracking. Alternatively, this may simply be a sign of the blasé attitude of the playwright and his court audience toward goods as familiar and abundant as porcelain wares, especially given the indifferent quality of the mass-produced stuff shipped to Southeast Asia, as evinced by the cargo recovered from shipwrecks.[5]

In any event, the wily admiral easily outwits the rulers of these "wee, far-flung kingdoms" by inviting them onboard his flagship so he can give them the matrix of porcelain for their very own: a dwarf specimen of the living tree upon which porcelain fruit grows. Unable to resist the temptation to gain such an expedient means of reproducing porcelain—of obtaining a "perennial root" to plant themselves— the rulers clamber aboard, only to be overpowered at once by the admiral's troops. The admiral mercifully spares their lives after they pledge submission and tribute to the great Ming dynasty, but, as one of the rulers grumbles: "We ended up without a single piece of porcelain and almost lost our heads." The play has fun with the naivety and greed of these island kings—who would really believe that porcelain grows on trees? But it also gets at the wonder and awe that the seemingly magical creation process of Chinese porcelain inspired across the early modern world.

That is, at least until the early eighteenth century, when the code of producing "hard paste" or "true" porcelain was cracked circa 1710 by alchemist-chemists laboring in the kingdom of Saxony, and the French Jesuit Father d'Entrecolles sent his letters (in 1712 and 1722) from the imperial kiln city of Jingdezhen detailing the complete process. In 1739, at the height of the European chinoiserie craze but before France had succeeded in birthing its own "true" porcelain, the *Ballet des Porcelaines*, also known as *The Teapot Prince*, had its premiere at the château de Morville outside Paris. As Meredith Martin deftly argues in her essay in this volume, both Caylus's ballet libretto and its fairy tale source simultaneously mask and reveal the European colonial ambition to acquire the magical secret of porcelain creation by beating the Chinese at their own game, by turning "China" into china.

The fantasy of unlimited generation of porcelain dramatized in *Voyage to the Western Ocean* forms a neat parallel with the ballet and the fairy tale. In the ballet, an evil sorcerer turns people into porcelain on his island kingdom, effectively killing them by dooming them to a living death, until finally the spell is broken, smashing the porcelain and transforming these decorative objects back into human beings. (In the fairy tale, the teapot prince turns himself into a weapon to attack the sorcerer, smashing himself in a simultaneous act of heroism and self-sacrifice, which miraculously turns the sorcerer's spell against him, transforming the sorcerer into a grotesque porcelain statue, a Chinese "pagod.") In these plots, gaining boundless mastery over porcelain manufacture is linked to the creative and destructive forces of life and death.

Building on recent scholarship that takes seriously the fantasmatic elements in Chinese accounts of transmutation in porcelain manufacture leads me to reposition the French ballet and the Ming opera within a subset of Chinese writings that imagine porcelain on the cusp between life and death, person and thing, animate and inanimate.

* * *

Sorcerers who transform people into inanimate objects are not typically found in Chinese tales. Instead, things themselves, especially old or worn-out quotidian ones, may shape-shift of their own volition to temporarily assume human guise and manifest themselves to ordinary people. Once rediscovered in their original form, smashing, burning, or burying these things suffices to exorcise their demonic spirits.[6] In the case of statues or paintings already fashioned in human form, no transformation of physical likeness is necessary, however, and it is typically the desire of the viewer that animates them and triggers the haunting.

One such Tang dynasty tale from the later eighth century is unusual because it involves a *porcelain* statue. The statue is not otherwise described except to say it was of "a young woman" and had stood in the household of a husband and wife for some time. One day, the wife teasingly says to the statue: "You should become my husband's concubine." As in folk tales worldwide, such jokes are dangerous because they may come true. The husband subsequently falls into a daze in which he keeps making love with a strange woman in his bed. The haunting is eventually traced back to the porcelain statue, whereupon "they smash it open and find blood inside its heart the size of a chicken egg."[7] The story doesn't explain further, but in

FIGURE 62

Liu Jianhua, Cup and Bowl from *Vessels*, 2009. Porcelain. Photo courtesy of Liujianhua Studio.

Chinese medicine, female blood and male essence are the organic matter required for reproduction. The uncanny implication here is that the statue is either in the early physiological process of becoming flesh or at an early stage of gestating a human embryo (the latter reinforced by the egg simile). Such inferences make sense in light of the long tradition of Chinese tales in which sex between a mortal man and supernatural woman may result in bringing her to life or giving birth to a human child.[8] But reading somewhat against the grain, could we interpret this story as a parable about the mesmerizing quality of porcelain as a material, the metamorphic process of its generation, and the extreme fragility of its bodily form?

* * *

What is clear is that porcelain manufacture was understood in Chinese terms as "an art of transformation," to borrow the title of Ellen Huang's superb article on "the mysterious, unintended, and even paranormal qualities" imbued in certain Qing dynasty glazes, and by extension, in Chinese porcelain production more generally.[9] In his letter of 1722, d'Entrecolles used the Chinese expression *yaobian* followed by the French gloss *transmutation* to describe a curious-looking piece of porcelain he had received from an artisan in Jingdezhen.[10] "Kiln transmutation," the literal meaning of *yaobian*, was a well-known phenomenon long attested to in Chinese texts, used for unexpected shapes, patterns, or colors discovered on ceramic pieces after firing—sometimes treated as demonic and unwanted, sometimes prized as rare and delightful. The late Ming connoisseur Gao Lian, who falls into the latter camp, offered this explanation in a manual of taste published circa 1591: *Yaobian* "are magical transformations wrought by high and low shifts in the fire; otherwise, the principle is unknowable, which would seem to make these effects even harder to obtain."[11]

But as Huang emphasizes, *yaobian* is also used in hagiographic accounts of male artisans or their female relatives voluntarily hurling themselves into the kiln, whose self-sacrifice effects the success of a difficult, desired result in the firing. Their bodies are literally transmuted into ceramic matter in the process. Such martyrs may be subsequently credited with certain technological innovations and worshipped as a *yaoshen*, the tutelary trade god of a kiln.[12] Red glazes in particular triggered such miracle tales not only because they were technically so challenging to produce, but also because of the visual similarity to blood. And blood, as we have already seen, is physically and symbolically linked to women; in most of these legends, it is the sacrificial blood of a young woman that transmogrifies in the kiln, giving her name to the glaze fused onto a vase and turning her into a goddess.[13] *Yaobian*, then, refers both to the mysterious, unpredictable forces at work in porcelain creation and to the deified artisanal creators whose self-destruction succeeds in controlling those forces.

It is easy for a viewer to imagine a connection between these legends about the transmogrification of human blood in the kiln and a large set of porcelain works simply entitled *Vessels* (2009) by the contemporary Chinese artist Liu Jianhua (b.

1962). In a cup and bowl from the series, inside and outside—white clay substrate and colored surface glaze—are dramatically reversed so that the red *sang-de-boeuf* glaze, shimmering like blood, literally becomes the contents of the porcelain vessels (Fig. 62).

* * *

The contemporary Chinese artist Geng Xue (b. 1983) brings together the many thematic strands of this essay in a short stop-motion animation film of a miniature world composed entirely of blue and white porcelain: trees, figures, flowers, scenic background, all made in Jingdezhen according to her own design, and all lit and shot to enhance the alluring, erotic materiality of porcelain, its luster and reflectiveness, its hardness and fragility (Fig. 63).[14] Composed by Wu Huanqing and Wang Jiyu, the film score is interspersed—like Sugar Vendil's music for the *Ballet des Porcelaines*—with the hap-

tic sound effects of tinkling, tapping, scratching, and cracking, adding to the visual illusion by immersing us in a sound world of porcelain. The film is based on a seventeenth-century fantastic tale from Pu Songling's magnum opus, *Strange Tales from a Chinese Studio*. The brief story Geng Xue chose, "Mr. Sea," is not a well-known one, but many elements overlap with the *Ballet des Porcelaines*: an enchanted island, a romance, and an evil sorcerer vanquished (here, a giant porcelain serpent patterned in blue and white, the "Mr. Sea" of the title).

Geng Xue harnesses the magic of animation to conjure up a tiny blue-and-white porcelain teapot and cup metamorphosing out of clay to serve the young man after he arrives on the island, and then to show the beautiful female inhabitant of the island emerging piece by piece out of a flaming saggar. It is love at first sight. In the midst of their lovemaking, the serpent approaches to claim his victim, and the woman abruptly smashes into pieces. Struggling for his life as the serpent starts extracting and drinking his blood, the young man finds himself staring at a broken fragment of his lover's face. He drops the fragment along with the poison from a blue-and-white vial into the puddle of red blood at his feet. This kills the serpent but unexpectedly shatters the man to bits. The film ends with a shot of him lying on the seashore "restored to life," an intact porcelain figure again. The violent history of porcelain's creative and destructive powers is once more concealed behind the material's smooth, shining, beautiful surface.

"Mr. Sea" and two pieces from *Vessels* will be on view at the Smart Museum of Art at the University of Chicago as part of the exhibition *Porcelain: Material and Storytelling*, curated by the art historian Wu Hung. It is timed to overlap with the University's performances of the *Ballet des Porcelaines*.

FIGURE 63

Film still from Geng Xue, *Mr. Sea*, 2014. Courtesy of the artist.

1 The play's full title is *Feng tianming Sanbao xia Xiyang* (Upon Imperial Command, Admiral Zheng Voyages to the Western Ocean). The version extant today is based on a "palace script" copy transcribed in 1615 as part of the Maiwangguan collection. My translations are keyed to *Xia Xiyang zaju* (Voyage to the Western Ocean, a Variety Play), edited and annotated by Xu Yuqiao (Xingzhou: Xingzhou shijie shuju, 1962). On the dating and interpretation of this play, see Roderich Ptak, "Sulu in Ming Drama," *Philippine Studies* 31 (1983): 227–42.

2 Liana Chen, *Staging for the Emperors: A History of Qing Court Theatre, 1683–1923* (Amherst, NY: Cambria Press, 2021), 144–45. She notes that although reference to Great Britain's mission to China is made in the preface to this opera, it may not have been actually performed on that occasion.

3 The earliest version of this type is a ballet libretto dated to 1600–1601, titled "Stanzas Written Hastily for the Ballet of the Princes of China." See Adrienne Ward, *Pagodas in Play: China on the Eighteenth-Century Italian Opera Stage* (Lewisburg, PA: Bucknell University Press, 2010), 68–69.

4 Second Demi-Act, *Xia Xiyang zaju*, 32–41.

5 For a fifteenth-century shipwreck in the Philippines, see Anne Gerritsen, *The City of Blue and White: Chinese Porcelain and the Early Modern World* (Cambridge: Cambridge University Press, 2020), 128–31.

6 See Judith T. Zeitlin, "The Ghosts of Things," in *Fantômes dans l'Extrême-Orient d'hier et d'aujourd'hui*, ed. Vincent Durand-Dastès and Marie Laureillard, 2 vols. (Paris: Presses de Inalco, 2017), 1: 205–21.

7 Li Fang et al., comps. "Lu Zanshan," in *Taiping guangji* (Wide Gleanings from the Taiping Reign) (Beijing: Zhonghua shuju, 1961), chap. 368, p. 2930, classified under "Miscellaneous Implements." For another haunting by a porcelain statue, described as a "courtesan with green glaze decoration," see "Liu Chong," p. 2931.

8 Judith T. Zeitlin, *The Phantom Heroine: Ghosts and Gender in Seventeenth-Century Chinese Literature* (Honolulu: University of Hawai'i Press, 2007), especially 32–37.

9 Ellen Huang, "An Art of Transformation: Reproducing *Yaobian* Glazes in Qing-Dynasty Porcelain," *Archives of Asian Art* 68, 2 (October 2018): 133–56, on 137.

10 Huang, "An Art of Transformation," 135. My treatment of yaobian is heavily indebted to Huang's discussion.

11 Gao Liao, "Lun Guan Ge yao qi" ("On Guan and Ge Ware"), in *Zunsheng bajian* (Eight Sets of Notes for Nourishing Life) (Lanzhou: Gansu wenhua chubashe, 2003), 337.

12 For a wonderful interpretation of an inscription and hagiography in the 1730s composed by Tang Ying, the famous superintendent of imperial kilns, commemorating the self-immolation of a late Ming artisan and promoting him as the "fire god" of Jingdezhen, see Zheng Yan, "Longgang yu wupen: qiwu zhong de ling yu rou" ("Dragon vat and black pot: spirit and body in vessels"), *Wenyi yanjiu* (October 2018), 113–28.

13 Zheng Yan, "Longgang yu wupen," 115 and 125, n. 25; Huang, "An Art of Transformation," 133 and 137–38.

14 In "Jingtou qian de diaosu" ("Sculpture in front of the lens"), a talk delivered in 2021, Geng Xue explains her aims and process in making the film. My thanks to Panpan Yang for introducing me to both the artist's film and this talk. See https://mp.weixin. qq.com/s/oqu3T0186giiHnRPdUDI8A (accessed November 21, 2021).

ELIZABETH ROUGET *Princeton University*

LIVING THINGS OR THE COLLECTOR AS AUDIENCE

Animate Porcelain Dancers

It is January 14, 1734, and Marie Sallé (1700–1756) has left her dancing shoes in the dressing room for a pair of sandals. Today she will premiere her first original work and dance the leading role. Dressed in a Greek chiton, without corset or pannier, she has prepared to dance the part of Galatea in a pantomime ballet based on Ovid's *Pygmalion*. At long last, it is her own choreography that will be danced on the London stage, and she has insisted that proper Greek costuming is key in communicating the pantomime. A tale of desire and metamorphosis, this popular melodrama displays Pygmalion's sculpting talents, and his infatuation for his subject that brings Galatea to life. Dancing as a statue that comes alive would be a challenge, she knew, but what better artistic medium than ballet to show the transfiguration of stone to flesh. It was the naturalistic elements that were so important to her portrayal. Free of the constraints of the corset, pannier, and heeled shoes, she would put her own plasticity on display and truly depict the human in the stone. Her performance of Galatea would need to capture the animate as well as the inanimate.

Princeton University Library's Special Collections is host to many treasures in various mediums from practically every time period. From canvas to coin, paper, and *objets d'art*, the vast holdings captivate researchers and treasure hunters alike. The Allison Delarue Collection consists of materials pertaining to dance history, such as photographs, manuscripts of memoirs, letters, prints, and, most important for our purpose, porcelain figurines. Allison Delarue was a member of the Princeton class of 1928 and later worked at McCarter Theatre in the town of Princeton. A keen dance historian and balletomane, he collected many pieces from the 1750s to 1980s, amassing a collection that he would later give to the university. There are many treasures, including drawings by Pablo Picasso, photographs of Mikhail

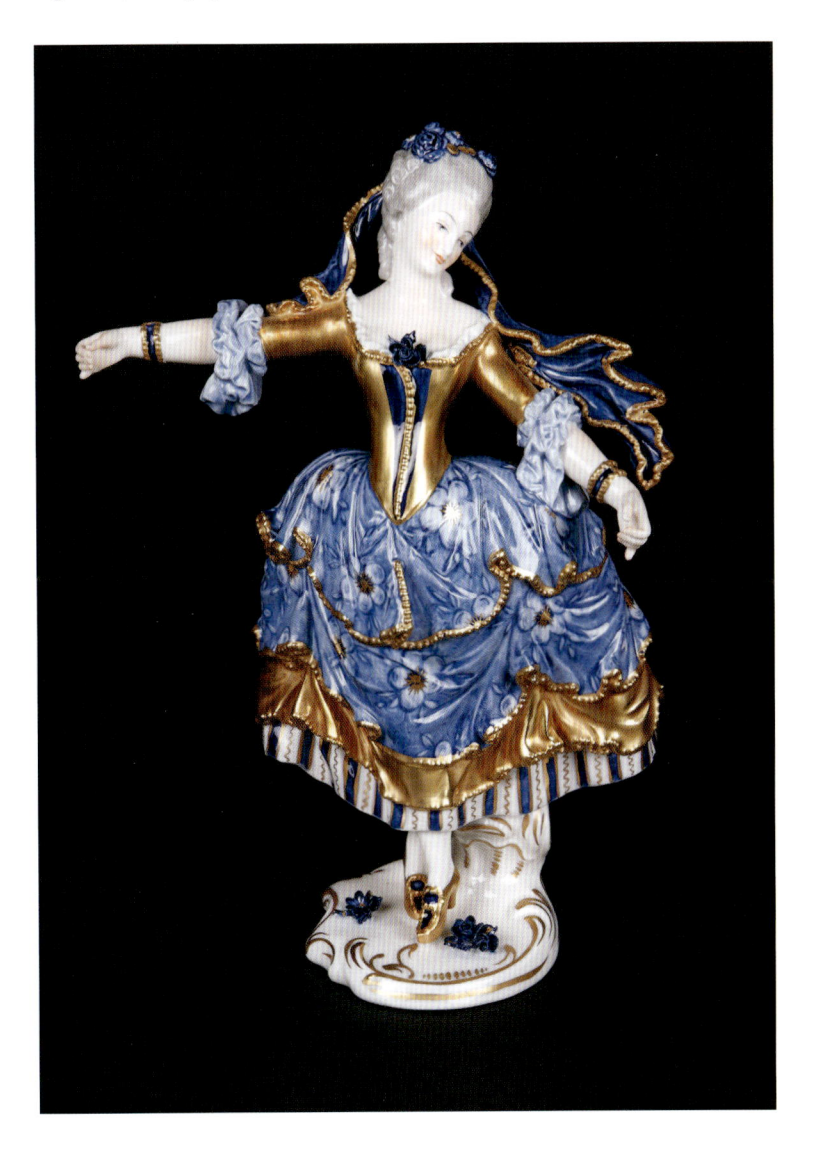

FIGURE 64

Marie Sallé, Twentieth-century German reproduction of a c. 1750 figure. Volkstedt-Rudolstadt manufactory, hard-paste porcelain, 24 × 17 × 10 cm. Allison Delarue Collection, William Seymour Theatre Collection. Special Collections, Princeton University Library. Image courtesy of Princeton University Library.

Baryshnikov and Martha Graham, prints of costumes for Tchaikovsky's ballets, and figurines of Fokine and Nijinsky, among others. Of the thirty-three porcelain models in the collection, five of them date from or are inspired by the eighteenth century, and to my delight, one is of Marie Sallé (Fig. 64). Made by the German porcelain manufactory Volkstedt-Rudolstadt, this twentieth-century reproduction echoes those figurines of Marie Sallé made by the Höchst Manufactory in the 1750s (an example of which is held at The Metropolitan Museum of Art). At Princeton, this delicate statue is dressed in a striking blue and gold dress, with gold dancing shoes and a blue veil. Her pose is daringly more dynamic than static, placing her in the midst of a ballet gesture, with arms open and head tilted to the side, as though her poised feet were about to leap in response to a lively musical passage. The veil flowing over her left shoulder is still in mid-rotation from her turn, as her feet gracefully cross one another. Her gaze follows and reaches beyond her extended left hand, leading us to imagine Marie advancing to the audience, and inviting us to partake of her delicate divertissement.

This figurine celebrates the skill required in shaping an inanimate object that mimics the movement of an animate one. Marie Sallé, as a vibrant dancer, is immortalized in porcelain as a living presence, frozen in a gesture normally fleeting and ephemeral, with fetching *épaulement*. Paradoxically, the pulse of baroque dance rests on the combination of a held pose under fermata before movement. In these moments of reprieve, all baroque dancers are, in this sense, statues, liberated with the down beat. Sallé's challenge in dancing Galatea in *Pygmalion* is here reversed. The sculptor must turn living flesh into statue, all the while maintaining her balletic fluidity. The practice of making porcelain figurines of stage performers was, of course, common in the eighteenth century, as evinced in the rich tradition of depicting stock characters from the *commedia dell'arte*. Usually highly colored and emotive, these personages were brought to life and reminded the collector of the folly the actors performed. But what of creating a figurine of a named and famed dancer? There are examples of statuettes of Marie Antoinette and other such prominent historical persons (one of Shakespeare is included in the Delarue collection), but to craft an artist in porcelain during her heyday and then again in the twentieth century seems to me to be a very special feat. In an effort to capture Marie Sallé's theatricality and distinct human features, the animate is imprisoned in the inanimate. We, the audience, must act as Pygmalion in order to revive the dancer from within her porcelain form.

In reconstructing and reimagining the *Ballet des Porcelaines*, Meredith Martin and Phil Chan have given life once again to a work that had been left by history to harden into stone. It is truly inspiring for music and dance scholars to have this work come to Princeton, where so many students in the performing arts are deciding how to treat historical materials. Instead of being paralyzed by details of historical accuracy, which we may never truly be able to grasp, an impression of the work is more than enough to encapsulate and vitalize its spirit. Just as Marie Sallé is captured in porcelain, we are delighted by the material artistic sources that remain. As historians of the performing arts, there is still part of us that hopes that Pygmalion may come along to bring about that metamorphosis, so that we may witness the performances we all long for.

A SMASH HIT IN THE MAKING

On a small island in the North Sea, increasingly isolated from the rest of the world, in a region known as Buckinghamshire, there lies an enchanted palace. With its distinctive roofs and staircase towers, it appears to have landed from France and to be assuming every possible architectural style all at once (Fig. 65). Inside is a stunning collection of porcelain—French, Chinese, German, *chinois*. Elephant-head vases with floppy ears and curling trunks, *potpourri* ships with billowing pennons.[1] China plates silently explode in mid-air over the dinner table, while in the library Princess Zirphile loses her head and gets it back only when Prince Acajou smashes every chamber pot in the kingdom (Fig. 66).[2] Who's to know whether once the last visitors have left and the curators have gone home to bed, the Meissen monkey orchestra[3] doesn't strike up a tune? In short, Waddesdon Manor is an ideal setting for the *Ballet des Porcelaines*, also known as *Le Prince Pot-à-Thé*.

Hosting Meredith Martin and Phil Chan's reimagining of the piece, we—Mia Jackson, curator of decorative arts at Waddesdon, and Kate Tunstall, professor

FIGURE 65

Aerial view of Waddesdon Manor.
Waddesdon Image Library.
Photo by John Bigelow Taylor, NYC.

of French in the University of Oxford—have received generous support from the Rothschild Foundation, the British Society for Eighteenth-Century Studies, and the Humanities Cultural Programme of The Oxford Research Centre for the Humanities (TORCH). There will also be a series of associated events, including baroque movement and rococo porcelain for children, and conversations between academics and creatives in the Sultan Nazrin Shah Centre, set in the gardens of Worcester College, Oxford.

On June 24, 1741, *Le Prince Pot-à-Thé* was reprised in the gardens of the château de Morville, where it had first been performed on September 20, 1739. The *parterre* and the pool were lit up for the occasion and surrounded by scenery in the shape of teacups, bowls, and vases, probably made of cardboard and perhaps with the dancers inside them. At the top of the pool in an illuminated archway stood a teapot. The prince or shepherd sets sail across the pool and no sooner lands on the shores of the mysterious island than a sorcerer turns him into a teapot. Nodding to *The*

FIGURE 66

Ingo Maurer, *Porca Miseria*, 2003. Porcelain, steel, and halogen light. Rothschild Foundation, Waddesdon (124. 2003). © Ingo Maurer GmbH, Munich. Waddesdon Image Library. Photo by Mike Fear.

Odyssey, the ballet gives the modern island voyager a fate not porcine but porcelain. It was the fate of some modern soldiers too: did Augustus the Strong not swap Frederick Wilhelm I of Prussia six hundred men for a hundred and fifty-one pieces of blue and white porcelain, known to this day as "dragoon vases"?

The ballet is based on an anonymous fairy tale published in 1731 that tells of the origins of the pagod, a porcelain figurine, usually wearing a floral robe barely covering his belly and a laughing expression; sometimes, thanks to a mechanism hidden from view, it could nod its head.[4] In the tale, it is the fate of the sorcerer to be turned into one such porcelain automaton. The princess, come to the island to rescue the prince, places him on the frame above the door to the sorcerer's bedroom. When he opens it, the teapot-prince comes crashing down on his head, knocks the sorcerer out, smashes himself into a thousand pieces, and returns to his handsome self. Just as the sorcerer is about to come round, he instead turns into a pagod, able only to nod his head, which he does as menacingly as he can while the prince and princess enjoy their wedding party, surrounded by their courtiers—formerly teacups and bowls and rollwagen vases. Judging by the surviving text, the nodding pagod did not make it into the ballet,[5] but the ornamentalized Oriental and the orientalized ornament would be common tropes of so much later European cultural production,[6] and the modern automaton, robot, or cyborg is all too often racialized as Asiatic.[7] If anyone can deploy an eighteenth-century *ballet-pantomime* to rescue us from these tropes and traps, Phil Chan can.

Following what will be the latest reprise of *Le Prince Pot-à-Thé*, this time in the gardens at Waddesdon in June 2022, Oxford will host a series of conversations responding to the piece: we imagine we will speak about porcelain-making and breaking, personhood, thingness, dance and race, technology and artificial intelligence—but let's wait and see the show.

---

[1] Svend Eriksen, *The James A. Rothschild Collection at Waddesdon Manor: Sèvres Porcelain* (Fribourg: Office du Livre, 1968), catalogue numbers 21, 43, 48, 49, 50, 51, 53.

[2] The book in question is Charles Duclos, *Acajou et Zirphile, conte* (Paris: A Minutie, 1744). The edition contains prints by Quentin-Pierre Chedel after François Boucher, originally done for another tale by the comte de Tessin. For more on the recycling of the images, see Tili Boon Cuillé, "Of Mind and Matter in Charles Duclos's *Acajou et Zirphile*," *Eighteenth-Century Fiction* 31, 1 (Fall 2018): 163–87.

[3] R. J. Charleston and John Ayers, *The James A. Rothschild Collection at Waddesdon Manor: Meissen and Oriental Porcelain* (Fribourg: Office du Livre, 1971), catalogue number 63.

[4] For more on pagods, see Danielle Kisluk-Grosheide, "The Reign of Magots and Pagodes," *The Metropolitan Museum Journal* 37 (2002): 177–97; and Kate E. Tunstall, "*Le neveu de Rameau*, règne des magots et des pagodes," *Diderot Studies* 35 (2015): 329–46.

[5] Nodding pagods do feature, however, in Rameau's comédie-ballet of 1760, *Les Paladins*. We know from the surviving maquette for Pietro Algieri's set design (see Fig. 22) that the palace in Act III contained numerous pagods, and the score makes it clear that when the magician commands, "Animez-vous," the pagods nod their heads ("meuvent leur tête dans la manière ordinaire"). See also R. Peter Wolf, "Rameau's *Les Paladins*: From Autograph to Production," *Early Modern Music* 11, 4 (1983): 497–504. In the 2004 production at Chaillot in Paris, the dancers did a virtuoso robotics routine: see https://www.youtube.com/watch?v=aX9K_KBVRjU (accessed November 15, 2021).

[6] Anne Anlin Cheng, *Ornamentalism* (Oxford: Oxford University Press, 2019).

[7] David S. Roh, Betsy Huang, and Greta A. Niu, eds., *Techno-Orientalism: Imagining Asia in Speculative Fiction, History, and Media* (New Brunswick, NJ: Rutgers University Press, 2015); Cheng, *Ornamentalism*.

ALEXANDRA LOSKE *Royal Pavilion & Museums Trust, Brighton & Hove*

A TEAPOT PRINCE AND HIS ENCHANTED PALACE

The Royal Pavilion, Brighton

In the early 1800s, the future King George IV (1762–1830; r. 1820–30) created a spectacular pleasure palace on England's south coast, the Royal Pavilion in Brighton (Figs. 68 and 69). The building's history actually began in 1787, when, as a young, fun-loving Prince of Wales, he built himself a small, elegant, neo-classical pavilion, with the aim of creating a party palace away from the strictures of London court life and his parents, King George III and Queen Charlotte.

Fifteen years later George began transforming this rather chaste-looking Marine Pavilion (as it was called then) into one of the most comprehensive manifestations of an early nineteenth-century European vision of the East. Using the skills and imagination of the interior decorators Robert Jones and John and Frederick Crace, George introduced Chinese-inspired interiors from 1802, and in 1815—after he had become Prince Regent—he engaged the equally excitable architect John Nash, who turned the exterior into what the essayist William Hazlitt mockingly described as "a collection of stone pumpkins and pepper-boxes."[1] It was also compared by some to the Kremlin—a curious misinterpretation of its Indian-inspired minarets, onion-shaped domes, and traceried balustrades.

By the early 1820s, the Pavilion's transformation was near-complete, and many contemporaries were in awe of this jewel-like building in the middle of a picturesque Regency garden, where newly imported colorful plants from China and India rubbed shoulders with English roses, trees, and shrubs. Although there were some critical and disdainful voices, many contemporaries expressed fascination and wonder at the sight of George's seaside palace, comparing it to a "fairy land"[2] or an enchanted palace from *One Thousand and One Nights*.[3]

Much has been said about George IV's alleged self-obsession, vanity, and fickleness, but he was also a generous man who had a refined taste in the arts. In British royal history, he is undoubtedly the greatest art collector, supporter, and patron.[4] His extraordinary pavilion by the sea was nearly lost: in 1850, his niece, Queen Victoria, sold it to Brighton Town Commissioners, although by then it was in a stripped and devastated state. Victoria had removed almost all the interiors in the preceding years, reusing many of the decorative objects, carpets, furniture, and fittings for Buckingham Palace. Much was returned over the decades, and recently a major temporary loan of more than 130 objects—most of them mounted Asian porcelain—from Her Majesty The Queen enabled visitors to experience George's vision in nearly complete form.[5] Since 2020, the Royal Pavilion and its associated museums and collections have formed an independent organization, the Royal Pavilion & Museums Trust. The Trust is determined to keep the Royal Pavilion at

FIGURE 67

After A. C. Pugin, The Music Room, Royal Pavilion, c. 1825, from John Nash's *Views of the Pavilion at Brighton*, 1826. Aquatint, 26.4 × 34.7 cm. Royal Pavilion & Museums Trust, Brighton & Hove. Detail of Fig. 69.

FIGURE 68

The West Front of the Royal Pavilion. Royal Pavilion & Museums Trust, Brighton & Hove. Photograph by Simon Dack, 2018.

the center of creative life in Brighton, showcasing the very best art and culture for as many people as possible.

Porcelain in the Royal Pavilion

George had many passions, and collecting colorful ceramics was one of his greatest. He amassed unparalleled quantities of Sèvres and Vincennes as well as Asian porcelain, which he used as moveable accents in his everchanging interior design schemes. His taste for *chinoiserie* and the exotic was partly inspired by female members of his family, especially his mother, Queen Charlotte (1744–1818). It is thought that she gave him a pair of exquisite Chinese vases when he was very young, which he displayed in his London palace Carlton House, and later moved to the Royal Pavilion. The Chinese and Japanese vases, bowls, figures, and pagodas acquired by George are spectacular examples of Asian export ware, boldly colored and often decorated with popular Chinese motifs such as mythical birds, dragons, bats, and chrysanthemums. Almost all of George's Asian porcelain was richly mounted in gilt bronze or otherwise embellished in Europe, with alterations and additions stemming from the Western imagination. He also owned several Chinese export figures known as "nodders" or "shakers," made of unfired clay and usually depicting high court officials.

After A. C. Pugin, The Music Room, Royal Pavilion, c. 1825, from John Nash's *Views of the Pavilion at Brighton*, 1826. Aquatint, 26.4 × 34.7 cm. Royal Pavilion & Museums Trust, Brighton & Hove.

The Music Room with two of the pagodas and other objects lent by H. M. The Queen in 2019. Royal Pavilion & Museums Trust, Brighton & Hove. Photograph by Jim Holden.

Undoubtedly the greatest examples of George's Asian porcelain objects are the six colossal porcelain Chinese towers, better known as pagodas, in the Royal Pavilion's Music Room (Fig. 69 and 70). They were probably made for him in China in the early nineteenth century, and brought from there by British East India Company ships. In England, George gave instructions for the pagodas to be embellished further, to fit the scale and glamour of the room. They were heightened with pedestals of English porcelain and scagliola, and topped with snake-entwined arrowheads and winged dragons. The four tallest pagodas eventually measured more than fifteen feet in height. Hundreds of Eastern-style gilded bells, dolphins, and dogs were added to them. The tiny bells must have added a delicate chiming sound when guests gathered and danced in the Music Room.

The extravagance displayed in Brighton and George's other residences did not go unnoticed, and in the 1820s caricaturists frequently associated his excesses with the Royal Pavilion. At times they depicted George resembling a grotesque porcelain figurine known as a pagod (for more on pagods, see Meredith Martin's essay in this volume). Sitting atop a large Chinese teapot in one such image, George looks like a cross between a teapot and one of his Pavilion's bulbous domes—a merciless satire of his costly art and architectural patronage (Fig. 71).

Many *chinoiserie* elements of the Royal Pavilion, and the Music Room in particular, were inspired by images of China created by William Alexander, an artist who, at the age of just twenty-five, was chosen to accompany Lord Macartney's 1792–94 embassy to China as a junior draughtsman. Alexander's carefully observed anthropological images and descriptions were widely disseminated in

FIGURE 71

Robert Seymour, "Shortshanks": *The Great Joss and his Playthings*, c. 1829. Hand-colored etching, 25.3 × 35.1 cm. Royal Pavilion & Museums Trust, Brighton & Hove.

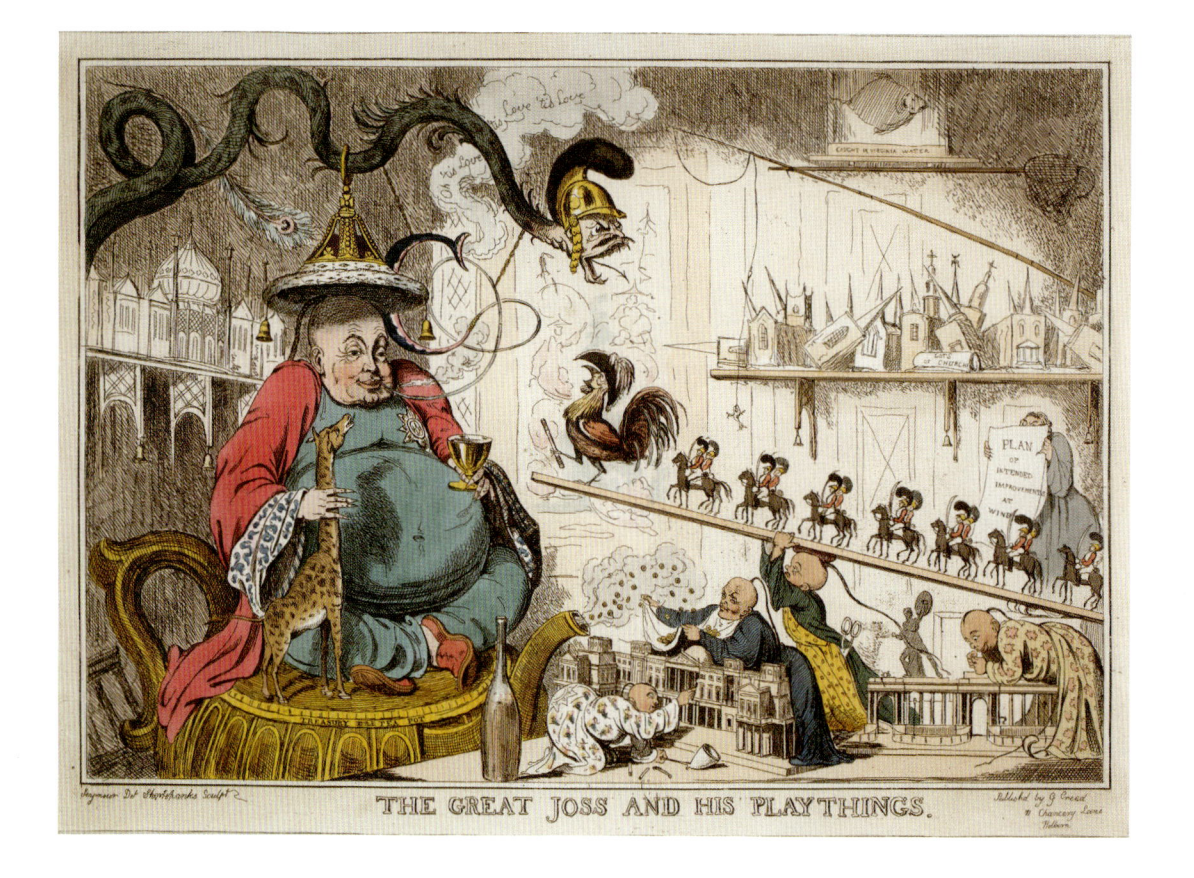

THE GREAT JOSS AND HIS PLAYTHINGS.

print form, and they shaped a new image of China through Western eyes in the early nineteenth century. George's designers John and Frederick Crace owned a copy of Alexander's illustrated book, *The Costume of China* (1805), from which they lifted numerous motifs, incorporating them into the landscape paintings on the Music Room walls, the chandeliers, and other decorative surfaces and objects in the building.[6]

The aim of the Macartney Embassy was to negotiate better trading conditions in China for the British. Although carefully planned, it turned out to be a diplomatic failure, as was the Amherst Mission in 1816. It is perhaps significant that George's bold and grandiose *chinoiserie* interiors at Brighton were created in the wake of these two failed missions and are indeed directly informed by them. However, we can only speculate as to whether George was trying to comment on these political and cultural tensions, since he has left not a single line of correspondence on the matter. It is hard to know, as Kara Blakley has suggested, whether George installed the Music Room pagodas and other objects in the Pavilion as "signifiers of Britain's imperial aspirations," but it is certainly a possibility.[7]

An intriguing comment from another source may corroborate Blakley's interpretation, but it dates from after George's death. In 1833, John Docwra Parry embedded a lengthy description of the Royal Pavilion in his *Historical and Descriptive Account of the Coast of Sussex*. Parry was one of the first writers to put George's seaside palace into a wider European context, by comparing its eclectic, "Oriental" style to other architectural fancies by Western rulers:

> And whilst the King of Saxony has his *Japanese Palace*, the Emperor of Austria his *Favorita*, and he of Russia his fanciful palaces of heterogeneous outline, whilst the Sovereign of England has in addition the noble and regular Gothic pile of Windsor, and the Roman palaces of London, we do not see why, if only for the sake of variety, he should not have his *Oriental Marine Pavilion*.[8]

Parry continues in an imperialist vein (although it should be noted that the king he refers to was George's successor, William IV):

> The King of England is almost "*de facto*" *King of India*; and, therefore, may we not say without fanciful exaggeration, that an eastern palace, placed on the shores of that element by the ancient and continual sovereignty of which England wields such a powerful sceptre, presents an idea to the mind, full, interesting, and effective.[9]

The Royal Pavilion is a building that draws you in, takes you on a journey, and tickles your senses. George's guests would have enjoyed a multisensory experience, with color and sparkle increasing the farther they progressed through the building. Soft, thick carpets muffled footsteps, but there would have been a cacophony of voices, the tinkling of crystals from the chandeliers, the clatter of the serving of food and drink, and of course, music. The state rooms were perfumed, and underfloor heating would have made the palace a cozy and at times overheated place.

A Moving Interior of Sound and Vision

Dinners, balls, and concerts were the most exciting social events at George's court, and at Brighton he created the most dazzling interiors for these occasions.

Dancing and music formed an important part of Georgian culture, both in public social life and at court. Brighton had two Assembly Rooms, one of them next door to the Royal Pavilion, but George's Music Room, where performances of the *Ballet des Porcelaines* (also known as *The Teapot Prince*) will be held in June 2022, outdid them in splendor (Fig. 69). Here, The King's Band performed works by Mozart, Handel, Meyerbeer, Cherubini, and Beethoven, as well as selections from Italian opera. George invited famous composers and musicians to Brighton, among them Gioachino Rossini, and was even known to sing or play the piano and cello himself.[10]

In the first complete account of the Royal Pavilion in 1838, Edward Brayley almost gave up trying to describe the Music Room: "No verbal description, however elaborate, can convey to the mind or imagination of the reader an appropriate idea of the magnificence of this apartment."[11] It is indeed enchanting. The color and surface shimmer of the walls may make visitors think that they have walked into a gigantic lacquer box, while simultaneously creating vast visual windows into a different, quasi-Chinese world. Waterlily-shaped chandeliers appear to float in midair, and the circular tent-like ceiling, decorated with more than 25,000 shimmering plaster scallop shells, seems to echo the movement of waltzing couples.

You might say that the Royal Pavilion was designed predominantly for entertainment. It is a magical, escapist place that, as Richard Sickelmore noted, "enchants the senses, and excites."[12] It gives expression to the vision of George, the admired and ridiculed "Teapot Prince." What better place to reimagine and perform the *Ballet des Porcelaines* in the twenty-first century than in this pleasure palace created for music, dance, and colorful porcelain?

[1]   William Hazlitt, *Notes of a Journey Through France and Italy* (London: Hunt and Clarke, 1826), 3.

[2]   Charles Walker, *Brighton and its Environs* (London: Printed for the author, Townsend, Powell, and Co., 1809), 3.

[3]   Richard Sickelmore, *The History of Brighton, From the Earliest Period to the Present Time* (Brighton: R. Sickelmore and Co., 1823), 24.

[4]   In 2019, a major exhibition at the Queen's Gallery, *George IV: Art and Spectacle*, celebrated George as a collector and patron of the arts. See Kate Heard and Kathryn Jones, eds., *George IV: Art and Spectacle*, exh. cat. (London: Royal Collection Trust, 2019).

[5]   David Beevers, *A Prince's Treasure: From Buckingham Palace to the Royal Pavilion*, exh. cat. (Brighton: Royal Pavilion & Brighton Museums, 2019). The exhibition ran from September 2019 until January 2022.

[6]   William Alexander, *The Costume of China. Illustrated in Forty-Eight Engravings* (London: William Miller, 1805).

[7]   Kara Blakley, "Domesticating Orientalism: Chinoiserie and the Pagodas of the Royal Pavilion, Brighton," *Australian and New Zealand Journal of Art* 18, 2 (2018): 206.

[8]   John Docwra Parry, *An Historical and Descriptive Account of the Coast of Sussex* (Brighton: Wright & Son and London: Longman & Co., 1833), 115–16.

[9]   Parry, *An Historical and Descriptive Account*, 116.

[10]   For a more detailed account on music in the Royal Pavilion, see David Beevers, "The Royal Pavilion at Brighton," in Heard and Jones, *George IV*, 139–51.

[11]   Edward Wedlake Brayley, *Illustrations of her Majesty's Palace at Brighton: Formerly the Pavilion, Executed by the Command of King George the Fourth, Under the Superintendence of John Nash. To Which is Prefixed a History of the Palace* (London: J. B. Nichols and Son, 1838), 3.

[12]   Sickelmore, *History of Brighton*, 28.

SYLVAIN BELLENGER AND SARAH K. KOZLOWSKI *Museo e Real Bosco di Capodimonte, Naples*

A PORCELAIN ROOM AND A TEAPOT PRINCE

Maria Amalia's Salottino di porcellana *and* Le Prince Pot-à-Thé *in Naples*

In the comte de Caylus's productions in 1739 and 1741 of the ballet he called *Le Prince Pot-à-Thé*, West met East, human dancers transformed into porcelain vessels, and shattered fragments magically came together again—all within the fiction of performances that took place at the château de Morville and its surrounding gardens. Between 1757 and 1759 in Naples, a team of ceramicists and other artisans brought into play similar dynamics between inside and outside, part and whole, nature and art, and exoticism and antiquity in an entire room of porcelain for Maria Amalia of Saxony, queen of Naples and granddaughter of Augustus the Strong, founder of the Meissen porcelain manufactory (Fig. 72).

In 1743, Maria Amalia and her husband, Charles of Bourbon, had established the Real Fabbrica di Capodimonte, which soon became one of Europe's most distingushed centers of porcelain production. For the queen's *Salottino di porcellana* at the Palace of Portici, the master modeler Giuseppe Gricci assembled three thousand individual pieces of porcelain over a wooden armature to sheath the walls of a small rectangular room, which was also fitted with French mirrors and crowned with a stucco ceiling modeled and painted to imitate the porcelain below. The decorative program comprises a fictive *rocaille* bower, hung with flowers and fruits and studded with pastoral scenes, all set against a white ground, as if the room were a painted porcelain vessel turned outside in.

In the room's *chinoiserie* pastoral scenes, figures in "Chinese" dress strike theatrical poses and hold or engage with props including parasols, scrolls, silks, and painted porcelain vessels (Fig. 73). In turn, these scenes, imagined in the French fashion of Boucher or Pillement, inspired the scenography and costumes of Giovanni Paisiello's opera *L'idolo cinese*, performed at Naples's Teatro San Carlo in 1767. The Bourbons' passion for *chinoiserie*—a fictional China seen from a Neapolitan perspective—informed not only the palace at Portici, where a second "Chinese Room" accompanied the *Salottino di porcellana*, but also Villa Favorita in Resina, near Naples, and above all the so-called Palazzina Cinese in Palermo.

At Portici, where the *Salottino di porcellana* was fitted with an inlaid marble floor in the antique style, the Bourbons' imagination of a distant East converged with their archeological interests in the deep past. In this connection, it is worth noting that the comte de Caylus had visited Naples during his travels in Italy in 1714-1715, and had even toured the first excavations of Herculaneum undertaken by the prince of Elboeuf. After his return to France, Caylus became renowned for his collection of antiquities and for his treatises on the arts of the Greek and Roman world. His *Mémoire sur la peinture à l'encaustique et sur la peinture à la cire* (1755), a detailed technical essay for artists based on his studies at Pompeii, enjoyed particular success. If it seems strange that an antiquarian should compose a ballet that allegorizes European desire for "white gold" and call his protagonist *Le Prince Pot-à-Thé*—which to the early modern French ear must have sounded like a pseudo-Chinese name—consider that, in the eighteenth century, both porcelain and wax painting represented an artistic quest for techniques of polychromy that could withstand the vicissitudes of time.

Transported from Portici to Naples in the nineteenth century, Maria Amalia's porcelain room is now a centerpiece of the collections of the Museo e Real Bosco di Capodimonte, together with an important collection of porcelain from the Real Fabbrica. To celebrate the museum's role as both a steward of cultural heritage and a place for the reimagination of the past in the present, Capodimonte will welcome Meredith Martin and Phil Chan's production of *The Teapot Prince* (also known as the *Ballet des Porcelaines*) in June 2022, bringing its porcelain collections to life through dance. The ballet will take place in the royal apartments, in the Bourbon ballroom whose decoration was inspired by the Roman paintings rediscovered in the ancient cities buried by Vesuvius. Co-presented with the Fondazione

FIGURE 72

Giovanni Battista Natali and Giuseppe Gricci, *Salottino di porcellana* for the Palazzo Portici (now at the Museo di Capodimonte in Naples), 1757–59. Image courtesy of the Ministero della Cultura / Museo e Real Bosco di Capodimonte.

Campania dei Festival, and as part of the program of the Campania Teatro Festival, the production in Naples will unite dancers from the New York City Ballet with musicians based in Naples. Aspects of the performance will be produced in collaboration with two of the ballet's European venues: Palazzo Grassi in Venice and the National Ceramics Museum in Sèvres.

To accompany the performances of the *Ballet des Porcelaines* in Naples, the Centro per la Storia dell'Arte e dell'Architettura delle Città Portuali "La Capraia," a research center at the heart of the Bosco di Capodimonte, will present a two-day program of site visits and lectures dedicated to the early modern history of porcelain rooms in a global context, with special focus on Maria Amalia's *Salottino di porcellana* and Capodimonte's porcelain collection, which is currently being reinstalled in ten *cabinets* located in the most beautiful rooms of the royal apartments. The program will explore the mobilities and materialities of porcelain and porcelain rooms from Europe to Persia to the eastern coast of Africa, and will trace interconnected practices of collecting and display across the early modern world. Speakers will include Angela Carola-Perrotti, Paola Giusti, Valter Luca De Bartolomeis, Meredith Martin, Prita Meier, and Julia Weber. Participants will gather on site at the Museo di Capodimonte, the Real Fabbrica di Capodimonte, and the Reggia di Portici. During these two days of presentations, which will also encompass close study of individual works and spirited conversation, the Museum and Bosco will become a laboratory for new understandings of the history of art—and of porcelain—as a global story of cultural encounter and exchange.

FIGURE 73

Detail of *chinoiserie* scene and Chinese inscriptions from the *Salottino di porcellana*. Images courtesy of the Ministero della Cultura / Museo e Real Bosco di Capodimonte.

PALAZZO GRASSI OR THE PAST REVISITED

The name of Venice, usually associated with the art of glass, appears rarely in connection with porcelain. What is less generally known is that the oldest Chinese vase ever introduced in Europe belongs to the Treasury of St. Mark's. The Venetian Republic, historically very receptive to artifacts from the Far East, was no exception to the fashion of chinaware overflowing Europe after the secret of hard-paste porcelain—until then jealously guarded by the Chinese—was finally disclosed, thanks in part to a French Jesuit missionary.

In the eighteenth century, Venice gave rise to the third hard-paste porcelain factory in Europe, after Meissen in Saxony and Du Paquier in Vienna. But the Vezzi manufactory, established in 1720, had a short lifespan, and very few samples of its production have survived (see Fig. 33). Not until the second half of the eighteenth century would the city regain a significant place in this field in Europe, when some ceramists from Saxony settled in Venice and managed to revive the trade. The most remarkable examples of Venetian porcelain were produced by Geminiano Cozzi, whose factory was established in 1765. His pieces account nowadays for some of the most remarkable artifacts in the collection of Ca' Rezzonico or Galleria Cini, alongside those made at Meissen or Sèvres.

Venice, whose culture is characterized in particular by an interest in the East and a penchant for disguise, was not immune to the *chinoiserie* trend in vogue across Europe throughout the century. As early as 1716, when the prince-elector of Saxony, Augustus the Strong, founder of the Meissen manufactory, paid a visit to the city, he was greeted by a Chinese-themed boat party. Painting did not escape the craze, as evidenced by the delicate illustrations in Venetian palaces such as Ca' Rezzonico or Palazzo Pisani Moretta—not to mention the extraordinary Chinese décor painted by Giandomenico Tiepolo at Villa Valmarana ai Nani. Theater and opera also drew inspiration from this fanciful exotism, notably Carlo Goldoni's *L'isola disabitata*, whose setting was a deserted Chinese island in the sea of Kamtkat-kà, and Carlo Gozzi's *Turandot*, set in Peking. Both works were presented in Venice in 1757 and 1762 at Teatro San Samuele, at the time within a stone's throw from Palazzo Grassi (though since destroyed).

Why welcome the *Ballet des Porcelaines* at Palazzo Grassi, attuned as the latter is to contemporary creation (Fig. 74)? It is surely not enough to summon the proximity of a lost theater, or of Ca' Rezzonico, which faces Palazzo Grassi on the other side of the Grand Canal—even though both buildings have in common the same architect, Giorgio Massari, who finished the first and entirely conceived the other. As a matter of fact, while completing Ca' Rezzonico in the 1750s, Massari proved amazingly versatile in his allegiance to Baldassare Longhena's exuberant baroque inspiration, if one considers the three generations' gap and Massari's personal

FIGURE 74

Grand Staircase of Palazzo Grassi, Venice.
© Palazzo Grassi. Photo by Matteo De Fina.

inclination toward neoclassical simplicity as denoted in the palazzo opposite. Another demonstration of Venetians' passion for masks . . .

The *Ballet des Porcelaines* as re-created by Meredith Martin and Phil Chan is not and could not have been a pastiche, nor a tentative historicist reconstruction of the ballet as it was featured at the château de Morville in 1739. The libretto, in fact, preserved today in two copies at the Bibliothèque nationale de France (Bibliothèque de l'Arsenal and Département des arts du spectacle), though providing the story and the music, does not bear precise indications of the scenography. The version that will be shown in Palazzo Grassi's atrium is a contemporary reinterpretation—in terms of choreography, music, costumes—of the ballet, a deliberate choice to plainly embed a creation of the twenty-first century in a frame loaded with history.

Palazzo Grassi is itself a palimpsest as such. Extensively remodeled in the nineteenth century, its aspect was further transformed over the course of the twentieth century. Sumptuously furnished by Count Cini for his son, and subsequently sold after the latter's accidental death, the palace was turned into an international center for fashion and costume. The Marinotti family covered its internal courtyard with a huge veil composed of thousands of spheres of all sizes, all of Murano glass, making it look like a diamond marquee. In the 1980s, the architect Gae Aulenti chose to remove this veil, giving the building much of its present appearance. When François Pinault purchased the palazzo for his own collection, Tadao Ando added his highly subtle intervention to the building while entirely reconstructing the Teatrino, a sort of contemporary re-creation of the old San Samuele theater that was once so famous. His work is invisible from the outside, hidden behind the old façade that has been left untouched.

Very recently, three large frescoes have been revealed at Palazzo Grassi, the creation of which is contemporaneous to the *Ballet des Porcelaines*. We owe these frescoes to Carlo Innocenzo Carloni, famous for the large decorative cycles he produced all over Central Europe, such as those at the Belvedere in Vienna. Removed by an antiques dealer from a villa near Bergamo, a practice still common during the last century, the frescoes were bought in 1950 by Franco Marinotti to adorn Palazzo Grassi, left empty after the removal of the Cini collections. After FIAT's acquisition of the palazzo in 1986, the frescoes were deposited and nearly forgotten for over thirty years. They celebrate in a series of three paintings the glory of the most famous condottiere of the Serenissima, Bartolomeo Colleoni, whose majestic equestrian statue stands proudly in front of the basilica of San Zanipolo.

The delicate restoration of these frescoes was opened to public view in autumn 2021 and treated as a contemporary cultural event, thanks to the all but theatrical scenography conceived by a team of young Venetian designers. The care that has been dedicated to this forgotten piece of heritage, passed down to us after being moved around from one context to another, is consistent with the vital intention to rethink art history in the light of today's concerns.

The re-creation of the *Ballet des Porcelaines* shares the same essential intention. Palazzo Grassi is, therefore, happy to be one of the destinations of this beautiful project and to welcome the *Teapot Prince*, who, departing New York, will cross the ocean, arrive in England, stop off in Naples, and reach Venice before a final performance in Sèvres.

THE SÈVRES MANUFACTORY

Three Centuries of a Ballet of Porcelain

For nearly three centuries, the Sèvres manufactory and its museum near Paris have preserved, enriched, and shared a unique heritage. A place of rich artistic and cultural life, Sèvres celebrates the medium of ceramics with a deep appreciation for its centuries-old forms and techniques, and for the beauty of works of art produced across the ages.

At the Sèvres manufactory, one hundred and twenty artisans work in nearly thirty distinct workshops, all exclusively manual and each with its own specialty, from the making of the porcelain pastes to the shaping of forms to the final decoration of the pieces (Figs. 75 and 76). In collaboration with invited artists and designers, the manufactory produces a rich array of objects in porcelain—jewelry, architectural elements, tableware, vases, light fixtures, furniture, sculpture—all distinguished by their originality and exceptional quality.

Established in the nineteenth century, the Sèvres museum is a source of inspiration for the manufactory's artisans, as well as for visitors, particularly artists, designers, and collectors. The first museum dedicated to ceramics, the earliest artistic medium, it currently conserves more than fifty thousand pieces, including Sèvres porcelain as well as the archives of the manufactory. Originating from all over the world and dating from all periods, these objects reflect the great diversity and expressive qualities of the medium.

Sèvres serves as something of a rejoinder to the ephemeral and the industrial, rejecting exclusion, ugliness, and uniformity, and sharing the values of a new art of living together. At Sèvres, porcelain is viewed as a noble material, one that nonetheless invites experimentation and travel in time and space. These same values are inherent in Phil Chan and Meredith Martin's new production of the *Ballet des Porcelaines*.

The *Ballet des Porcelaines* reflects Sèvres's mission to impart the living tradition of ceramics and to enrich its dialogue with the arts through a multidisciplinary program of exhibitions and cultural and educational events. There are quite a few parallels between the making of porcelain and dance, perhaps chief among them the fact that both are exacting arts that entail repetition, precision, and time in order to appear effortless. At the manufactory, we often say that looking at the movements of the artisans at work is like watching a ballet of hands and bodies moving with confidence and precision from one step—one craft, one workshop—to another, each essential to the realization of the final work.

Furthermore, the *Ballet des Porcelaines* resonates with the early history of the Sèvres manufactory, which was created in 1740—just a year after the first performance of the ballet at the château de Morville—when a small workshop was established on the premises of the château de Vincennes. In 1756 the factory moved to Sèvres, halfway between the royal castles of the Tuileries and Versailles. It became first a royal manufactory in 1759 and then an imperial and national manufactory, dependent upon the political regimes that succeeded in France but always closely related to the French State.

The reputation of the Sèvres manufactory was established largely through its production of small sculptures, called biscuits. During the early years at Vincennes, they were covered by a brilliant, transparent glaze that allowed the whiteness of the paste to shine through, much like the "China Whites" that were then coveted by collectors in Europe. However, the glaze proved problematic for the young institution, as it tended to run during firing, leaving certain areas bare and dull while pooling in hollows and forming unsightly murky sections. This is doubtless one of the reasons why the decision was made, in about 1751–52, to leave the sculptures in a state of "biscuit"—that is, without a glaze. This set the Sèvres manufactory apart from its European rivals—which continued to produce enameled and colored figurines—and certainly contributed to its international reputation. Interestingly, this change took place at the moment when porcelain statuettes were starting to replace items in sugar or almond paste in table decoration. First produced by Meissen, this type of decoration in porcelain became immediately popular in Paris. The Vincennes manufactory was all the more eager to produce such figurines, as it was well known in France that the king, Louis XV, had ordered this type of decoration from Saxony.

In the 1750s, many porcelain sculptures made at Vincennes, and then at Sèvres, were executed after designs by the celebrated French painter François Boucher. These depicted pastoral scenes, as well as children dressed like adults playing at being peasants, hunters, dancers, and musicians. Several sculptures were inspired by *Les Vendanges de Tempé* (*The Harvest in the Vale of Tempé*), a 1745 play by Charles-Simon Favart, reconceived in 1752 as *La Vallée de Montmorency* (*The Montmorency Valley*) (Fig. 77). Boucher was a friend of Favart's and designed the sets for the play. During the following decades, contemporary theater and dance—whether comic opera or plays and ballets staged on the theaters of the Parisian boulevards and in private venues like the château de Morville—continued to be sources of inspiration for Sèvres biscuits. Such performances were, for example, the inspiration for *La Fête du château* (*The Chateau Celebration*) and its pendant, *La Fée Urgèle* (*Urgèle the Fairy*). Sèvres continued to demonstrate its strong ties to the theater by making portraits of famous actors in celebrated roles. The first dates to 1775, depicting the actor Préville (Pierre-Louis Dubus, 1721–1799) in the role of Figaro in *The Barber of Seville*. Other actors and actresses were immortalized by Sèvres throughout the eighteenth century, among them Sophie Forest in *La Pélerine* and Julie Candeille in *La Provençale*.

During the eighteenth century, Vincennes and Sèvres biscuits were placed atop tables, chimneypieces, chests of drawers, and other flat surfaces in the salons and boudoirs of the sophisticated residences of the king and his court. These provided topics of conversation for guests—especially the Sèvres pieces produced at the time of, or closely after, the related theatrical production. In the following centuries, these delicate small groups, which were found in the homes of collectors and on the shelves of museums all around the world, came to embody the production of the celebrated Sèvres manufactory. Outside the circle of a few avid collectors and experts, however, they are today mostly associated with a period long gone. The *Ballet des Porcelaines* invites us to newly engage with them as it brings porcelain figures to life.

Finally, Sèvres is particularly excited to be part of the international tour of the *Ballet des Porcelaines*, as it fulfills a wish dear to the institution to establish closer ties with cultural institutions in France and abroad, whether or not they have an exclusive focus on ceramics.

FIGURE 75

Painting and gilding workshops at the Sèvres Manufactory, Sèvres–Manufacture et musée nationaux. Photo courtesy of Gerard Jonca.

FIGURE 76

Painting and gilding a plate at the Sèvres Manufactory, Sèvres–Manufacture et musée nationaux. Photo courtesy of Gerard Jonca.

FIGURE 77

The Grape Eaters, c. 1757–66. Modeled under Etienne-Maurice Falconet after engravings by François Boucher, Sèvres manufactory, soft-paste biscuit porcelain, 22.9 x 24.8 x 17.8 cm. J. Paul Getty Museum, Los Angeles. Digital image courtesy of the Getty's Open Content Program.

———. *Choreography and Narrative: Ballet's Staging of Story and Desire*. Bloomington and Indianapolis: Indiana University Press, 1996.

Fourny, Diane. "A Strange Familiarity: Monkeys and Chinamen in Enlightenment France," *The French Review* 92, 4 (May 2019): 157–74.

Fumaroli, Marc. "Un gentilhomme universel: Anne-Claude de Thubières, comte de Caylus," in Joanot Martorell, *Tirant Le Blanc*, 563–81. Paris: Gallimard, 1997.

Garnier-Pelle, Nicole, and Monelle Hayot. *Les singeries du château de Chantilly = The Monkey Rooms*. Paris: Nicolas Chaudun, 2013.

Gerritsen, Anne. *The City of Blue and White: Chinese Porcelain and the Early Modern World*. Cambridge: Cambridge University Press, 2020.

Gerritsen, Anne, and Stephen McDowall. "Material Culture and the Other: European Encounters with Chinese Porcelain, ca. 1650–1850," *Journal of World History* 23, 1 (2012): 87–113.

Gleeson, Janet. *The Arcanum: The Extraordinary True Story*. London: Bantam, 1998.

Glorieux, Guillaume. *À l'enseigne de Gersaint. Edmé-François Gersaint, marchand d'art sur le pont Notre-Dame (1694–1750)*. Seyssel: Champ vallon, 2002.

Godenne, Réné. "Un inédit de Caylus: *Les Âges ou la fée du Loreau*, comédie en prose en un acte (1739)," *Studies on Voltaire and the Eighteenth Century* 106 (1973): 175–224.

Guichard, Charlotte. *Colonial Watteau: Commerce, Galanterie and Colonial Imagination in Regency France*. Berlin and Munich: Deutscher Kunstverlag, 2022.

———. "Connoisseurship: Art and Antiquities," in Colin Jones, Juliet Carey, and Emily Richardson, eds., *The Saint-Aubin Livre de caricatures: Drawing Satire in Eighteenth-Century Paris*, 292–309. Oxford: Voltaire Foundation, 2012.

———. "Taste Communities: The Rise of the 'Amateur' in Eighteenth-Century Paris," *Eighteenth Century Studies* 45, 4 (Summer 2012): 519–47.

Haifeng, Ni, and Marianne Brouwer. "A Zero Degree of Writing and Other Subversive Moments: An Interview with Ni Haifeng," in Roel Arkesteijn and Ni Haifeng, *Ni Haifeng: No-Man's Land*, 247–61. Amsterdam: Artimo, 2003.

Harris-Warrick, Rebecca, and Carol G. Marsh, *Musical Theatre at the Court of Louis XIV: Le Mariage de la Grosse Cathos*. Cambridge: Cambridge University Press, 2005.

Hartman, Saidiya. "Venus in Two Acts," *Small Axe* 26 (June 2008): 1–14.

Hattori, Cordélia. "Le comte de Caylus d'après les archives," *Les Cahiers d'histoire de l'art* 5 (2007): 54–70.

Hazlitt, William. *Notes of a Journey Through France and Italy*. London: Hunt and Clarke, 1826.

Henry, Charles. "Le comte de Caylus inédit," *La Revue libérale* (July 1884): 127–42.

Holmes, Mary Tavener. *Nicolas Lancret: Dance Before a Fountain*. Los Angeles: The J. Paul Getty Museum, 2006.

Holmes, Mary Tavener, and Joseph Focarino. *Nicolas Lancret: 1690–1743*. New York: Harry N. Abrams, 1991.

Hornback, Robert. *Racism and Early Blackface Comic Traditions: From the Old World to the New*. Cham, Switzerland: Palgrave Macmillan, 2018.

Huang, Ellen. "An Art of Transformation: Reproducing Yaobian Glazes in Qing-Dynasty Porcelain," *Archives of Asian Art* 68, 2 (October 2018): 133–56.

"Inventaire après décès de Charles Jean-Baptiste Fleriau, comte de Morville (1732)," Archives nationales de France (hereafter AN), 6AP/10.

"Inventaire après décès de Jeanne Gilbert, madame d'Armenonville (1716)," AN, 6AP/12.

Johns, Christopher. *China and the Church: Chinoiserie in Global Context*. Oakland: University of California Press, 2016.

Jones, Christine A. *Shapely Bodies: The Image of Porcelain in Eighteenth-Century France*. Newark: University of Delaware Press, 2013.

Kang, Angela. "Musical Chinoiserie." PhD dissertation, University of Nottingham, UK, 2005.

Keevak, Michael. *Becoming Yellow: A Short History of Racial Thinking*. Princeton: Princeton University Press, 2011.

Khelissa, Anne Perrin. "Menace sur le 'grand' art. Le peuple des magots et des statuettes en porcelaine au Siècle des Lumières," in Sophie Duhem, Estelle Galbois, and Anne Perrin Khelissa, eds., *Penser le 'petit' de l'Antiquité au premier xxe siècle: Approches textuelles et pratiques de la miniaturisation artistique*, 88–98. Lyon: Fage, 2017.

Kisluk-Grosheide, Daniëlle. "The Reign of Magots and Pagods," *Metropolitan Museum Journal* 37 (2002): 177–97.

L'Abbé, Anthony. *A New Collection of Dances*. London: F. Le Rousseau, c. 1725.

Lancelot, Francine. *La Belle Danse*. Paris: Van Dieren Éditeur, 1996.

Lau, Kimberly J. "Imperial Marvels: Race and the Colonial Imagination in the Fairy Tales of Madame d'Aulnoy," *Narrative Culture* 3, 2 (Fall 2016): 141–79.

Le Comte, Louis. *Memoirs and Observations Topographical, Physical, Mathematical, Mechanical, Natural, Civil, and Ecclesiastical, Made in a Late Journey Through the Empire of China . . . .* London: Benj. Tooke and Sam. Buckley, 1697.

Le Corbeiller, Clare. "Saint-Cloud and the 'Goust de Raphaël'," in Bertrand Rondot, ed., *Discovering the Secrets of Soft-Paste Porcelain at The Saint-Cloud Manufactory, ca. 1690–1766*, 43–46. New Haven: Yale University Press, 1999.

Le Gentil de La Barbinais. *Nouveau Voyage Autour du Monde*. Paris: Briasson, 1728.

Les Magots, parodie de "L'Orphelin de la Chine," en vers, en 1 acte. Paris: Vve Delormel et fils, 1756.

Li Fang et al., comps. "Lu Zanshan," in *Taiping guangji (Wide gleanings from the Taiping reign)*. Beijing: Zhonghua shuju, 1961.

Liao, Gao. "Lun Guan Ge yao qi" ("On Guan and Ge Ware"), in *Zunsheng bajian (Eight Sets of Notes for Nourishing Life)*. Lanzhou: Gansu wenhua chubashe, 2003.

Lilti, Antoine. *Le monde des salons: sociabilité et mondanité à Paris au XVIIIe siècle*. Paris: Fayard, 2005.

Littré, Émile. *Dictionnaire de la langue française*. Paris: Hachette, 1873, vol. 1, The ARTFL Project, https://artflsrv03.uchicago.edu/philologic4/publicdicos/uery?report=bibliography&head=canarie&start=0&end=0.

Mailly, chevalier de (?). *Le prince Perinet ou l'origine des Pagodes*, in *Le cabinet des fees, ou collection choisie des contes de fees, et autres contes merveilleux*, vol. 31, 205–32. Amsterdam and Paris: Rue et Hôtel Serpente, 1786.

Martin, Meredith. "Mirror Reflections: Louis XIV, Phra Narai, and the Material Culture of Kingship," *Art History* 38, 4 (September 2015): 652–67.

Martin, Meredith, and Gillian Weiss. "Enslaved Muslims at the Sun King's Court," in Mark Ledbury and Robert Wellington, eds., *The Versailles Effect: Objects, Lives, and Afterlives of the Domaine*, 153–76. London: Bloomsbury Visual Arts, 2020.

"Mémoire envoyé au comte de Morville sur le commerce des Indes et de la mer du Sud," AN, MAR/B/7/118, fols. 119–22, 29 juillet 1724.

Menzhausen, Ingelore. *Early Meissen Porcelain in Dresden*. New York: Thames and Hudson, 1990.

Mercure galant (February 1700).

Moehlenpah, Amanda. "'Les assemblées qu'elle occasionne': Danced Sociability in Eighteenth-Century France," *Eighteenth-Century Studies* 54, 3 (Spring 2021): 577–92.

Morrison, Simon. *Russian Opera and the Symbolist Movement*. 2nd ed. Oakland: University of California Press, 2019.

Mouat, Anne, and Melissa Mouat. "European Perceptions of Chinese Culture as Represented on the Eighteenth-Century Ballet Stage," *Music in Art* 38, 1–2 (Spring-Fall 2013): 49–61.

Munger, Jeffrey. *European Porcelain in The Metropolitan Museum of Art*. New York: The Metropolitan Museum of Art, and New Haven and London: Yale University Press, 2018.

Munger, Jeffrey, and Selma Schwartz. "Gifts of Meissen Porcelain to the French Court, 1728–50," in Cassidy-Geiger, ed., *Fragile Diplomacy*, 141–74.

Murdoch, Tessa. "Les cabinets de porcelaines," in Brunel, ed., *Pagodes et Dragons*, 42–49.

Ou, Hsin-Yun. "*The Chinese Festival* and the Eighteenth-Century London Audience," *The Wenshan Review of Literature and Culture* 2, 1 (December 2008): 31–52.

Palmer, Jennifer L. *Intimate Bonds: Family and Slavery in the French Atlantic*. Philadelphia: University of Pennsylvania Press, 2016.

Park, Julie. *The Self and It: Novel Objects in Eighteenth-Century England*. Stanford: Stanford University Press, 2010.

Parry, John Docwra. *An Historical and Descriptive Account of the Coast of Sussex*. Brighton: Wright & Son and London: Longman & Co., 1833.

Peabody, Sue. *"There Are No Slaves in France": The Political Culture of Race and Slavery in the Ancien Régime*. New York: Oxford University Press, 1996.

Pietsch, Ulrich, and Claudia Banz, eds. *Triumph of the Blue Swords: Meissen Porcelain for Aristocracy and Bourgeoisie 1710–1815*, exh. cat. Leipzig: E. A. Seeman and Dresden: Staatliche Kunstsammlungen Dresden Porzellansammlung, 2010.

Pietsch, Ulrich, and Theresa Witting, eds. *Fascination of Fragility: Masterpieces of European Porcelain*, exh. cat. Leipzig: E. A. Seemann and Dresden: Staatliche Kunstsammlungen Dresden, 2010.

Plagnol-Diéval, Marie-Emmanuelle. "Caylus et le théâtre de société: Morville, 1739–1740," in Cronk and Peeters, eds., *Le comte de Caylus*, 179–90.

"Plainte d'Anne-Catherine Desmares contre son mari Antoine-François Botot dit Dangeville, qui l'avait battue et injuriée (November 16, 1725)," reprinted in Émile Campardon, *Les Comédiens du roi de la troupe française pendant des deux derniers siècles*. Paris: Chez H. Champion, 1879.

Pollard, A. M. "Letters from China: A History of the Origins of the Chemical Analysis of Ceramics," *Ambix* 62, 1 (2015): 50–71.

Préaud, Tamara, and Antoine d'Albis. *La porcelaine de Vincennes*. Paris: Adam Biro, 1991.

Pritchard, James. "The Naval Career of a Colonial Governor: Charles de Thubières, Marquis de Caylus, 1698–1750," *Proceedings of the Meeting of the French Colonial History Society* 16 (1992): 12–23.

"Procés verbal de vente des meubles après le décès de Monseigneur d'Armenonville." AN, 6AP/10.

Pruiksma, Rose. "Of Dancing Girls and *Sarabandes*: Music, Dance, and Desire in Court Ballet, 1651–1669," *The Journal of Musicology* 35, 2 (2018): 145–82.

Ptak, Roderich. "Sulu in Ming Drama," *Philippine Studies* 31 (1983): 227–42.

Pullins, David. "L'introuvable peinture chinoise de François Boucher ou la question de la caricature," in Rimaud, ed., *Une des provinces du rococo*, 122–31.

———. "Techniques of the Body: Viewing the Arts and Métiers of France from the Workshop of Nicolas I and Nicolas II de Larmessin," *Oxford Art Journal* 37, 2 (2014): 135–55.

Quélus (Jean-Baptiste Caylus?). *Histoire naturelle du cacao et du sucre*. Paris: L. d'Houry, 1719.

Quéro, Dominique. "De la 'société de Morville' au 'théâtre du château de Morville'," in Quéro, ed., *Théâtre de société du comte de Caylus*, 11–52.

———, ed. *Théâtre de société du comte de Caylus: Comédies jouées au château de Morville (1738–1740)*. Reims: Université de Reims Champagne-Ardenne, 2016.

Ravel, Jeff. "The Coachman's Bare Rump: An Eighteenth-Century French Cover-Up," *Eighteenth-Century Studies* 40, 2 (Winter 2007): 279–308.

Report on the Manuscripts of Lady Du Cane. London: Ben Johnson and Co., 1905.

Rimaud, Yohan, ed. *Une des provinces du rococo: La Chine rêvée de François Boucher*, exh. cat. Besançon: Musée des beaux-arts et d'archéologie, 2019.

Rizzoni, Nathalie. "*Le Prince Pot à thé* de Caylus, de la porcelaine à la pantomime," in Quéro, ed., *Théâtre de société du comte de Caylus*, 449–73.

Roh, David S., Betsy Huang, and Greta A. Niu, eds. *Techno-Orientalism: Imagining Asia in Speculative Fiction, History, and Media*. New Brunswick, NJ: Rutgers University Press, 2015.

Rondot, Bertrand, ed. *Discovering the Secrets of Soft-Paste Porcelain at The Saint-Cloud Manufactory, ca. 1690–1766*, exh. cat. New Haven and London: Published for The Bard Graduate Center for the Studies in the Decorative Arts by Yale University Press, 1999.

———. "The Saint-Cloud Porcelain Factory," in Pietsch and Witting, *Fascination of Fragility*, 42–49.

Sago, Kylie. "Colonial Encounters of 'La Belle et la Bête'," in Jérôme Brillaud and Virginie Greene, eds., *Encounters in the Arts, Literature, and Philosophy: Chance and Choice*, 59–69. London: Bloomsbury Academic, 2021.

Scott, Katie. "Hierarchy, Liberty and Order: Languages of Art and Institutional Conflict in Paris (1766–1776)," *Oxford Art Journal* 12, 2 (1989): 59–70.

——. "Playing Games with Otherness: Watteau's Chinese Cabinet at the Château de la Muette," *Journal of the Warburg and Courtauld Institutes* 66 (2003): 189–248.

——. *The Rococo Interior: Decoration and Social Spaces in Early Eighteenth-Century Paris*. New Haven and London: Yale University Press, 1995.

Sheriff, Mary. *Enchanted Islands: Picturing the Allure of Conquest in Eighteenth-Century France*. Chicago: The University of Chicago Press, 2018.

Sickelmore, Richard. *The History of Brighton, From the Earliest Period to the Present Time*. Brighton: R. Sickelmore and Co., 1823.

Sloboda, Stacey. "Chinoiserie: A Global Style," in Christine Guth, ed., *Encyclopedia of Asian Design, vol. 4: Transnational and Global Issues in Asian Design*, 143–54. London: Bloomsbury Academic, 2018.

——. "Fashioning Bluestocking Conversation: Elizabeth Montagu's Chinese Room," in Denise Baxter and Meredith Martin, eds., *Architectural Space in Eighteenth-Century Europe: Constructing Identities and Interiors*, 129–48. Farnham, UK: Ashgate, 2010.

Smentek, Kristel. *Rococo Exotic: French Mounted Porcelain and the Allure of the East*. New York: The Frick Collection, 2007.

"Sommaire des maximes et des vues du marquis de Caylus dans l'administration des Isles françoises du Vent de l'Amérique et des lettres qu'il a écrit en consequence (1749)," *Archives nationales d'outre mer*, COL C8 A 58.

Stein, Perrin. "Les chinoiseries de Boucher et leurs sources: l'art de l'appropriation," in Brunel, ed., *Pagodes et Dragons*, 86–100.

——. "Vases and Satire," in Jones et al., eds., *The Saint-Aubin* Livre de caricatures, 310–33.

Steiner, Benjamin. *Building the French Empire, 1600–1800: Colonialism and Material Culture*. Manchester: Manchester University Press, 2020.

Swain, Virginia E. "Beauty's Chambers: Mixed Styles and Mixed Messages in Villeneuve's *Beauty and the Beast*," *Marvels & Tales* 19, 2 (2005): 197–223.

Tang, Guo. "De l'artifice au réalisme: L'évolution des 'chinoiseries' théâtrales dans la première moitié du 18e siècle," *Dix-huitième siècle* 49, 1 (2017): 645–59.

Tunstall, Kate E. "*Le neveu de Rameau*, règne des magots et des pagodes," *Diderot Studies* 35 (2015): 329–46.

Van Orden, Kate. *Music, Discipline, and Arms in Early Modern France*. Chicago: The University of Chicago Press, 2005.

Viala, Alain. *La France galante: Essai historique sur une catégorie culturelle, de ses origines jusqu'à la Révolution*. Paris: Presses Universitaires de France, 2008.

Vigarello, Georges. "The Upward Training of the Body from the Age of Chivalry to Court Civility," in Michel Feher, Ramona Naddaf, and Nadia Tazi, eds., *Fragments for a History of the Human Body*, vol. 2, 148–99. New York: Zone, 1989.

Volk, Cynthia. "Dehua Porcelain Figures of Budai: Models of Adaptivity in Seventeenth- and Eighteenth-Century China and 'Europe'." MA thesis, Bard Graduate Center, 2021.

Walcha, Otto. *Meissen Porcelain*. New York: Putnam Pub Group, 1981.

Walker, Charles. *Brighton and its Environs*. London: Printed for the author, Townsend, Powell, and Co., 1809.

Ward, Adrienne. *Pagodas in Play: China on the Eighteenth-Century Italian Opera Stage*. Lewisburg: Bucknell University Press, 2010.

Welch, Ellen R. "Dancing the Nation: Performing France in the Seventeenth-Century 'Ballet des nations'," *Journal for Early Modern Cultural Studies* 13, 2 (Spring 2013): 3–23.

——. *A Theater of Diplomacy: International Relations and the Performing Arts in Early Modern France*. Philadelphia: University of Pennsylvania Press, 2017.

Wiley, Roland John. "Dances in Opera: St. Petersburg," *Dance Research* 33, 2 (Winter 2015): 227–57.

Wolf, R. Peter. "Rameau's *Les Paladins*: From Autograph to Production," *Early Modern Music* 11, 4 (1983): 497–504.

Xue, Geng. "Jingtou qian de diaosu" ("Sculpture in front of the lens"), a talk delivered in 2021, https://mp.weixin. qq.com/s/0qu3T0186giiHnRPdUDI8A.

Yale University, Irving S. Gilmore Music Library. "Basic Glossary of Musical Forms," https://web.library.yale.edu/ cataloging/music/Basic-glossary-of-musical-terms.

Yan, Zheng. "Longgang yu wupen: qiwu Zhong de ling yu rou" ("Dragon Vat and Black Pot: spirit and body in vessels"), *Wenyi yanjiu* (October 2018): 113–28.

Yang, Chi-ming. "*Elephantine Chinoiserie and Asian Whiteness*: Views on a Pair of Sèvres Vases," *The Journal of the Walters Art Museum* 75 (2021), https://journal.thewalters. org/2021/05/elephantine-chinoiserie-and-asian-whiteness-views-on-a-pair-of-sevres-vases/.

——. *Performing China: Virtue: Commerce, and Orientalism in Eighteenth-Century England, 1660–1760*. Baltimore: Johns Hopkins University Press, 2011.

Yuqiao, Xu, ed. *Xia Xiyang zaju* (*Voyage to the Western Ocean, a Variety Play*). Xingzhou: Xingzhou shijie shuju, 1962.

Zeitlin, Judith T. "The Ghosts of Things," in Vincent Durand-Dastès and Marie Laureillard, eds., *Fantômes dans l'Extrême-Orient d'hier et d'aujourd'hui*, vol. 1, 205–21. Paris: Presses de Inalco, 2017.

——. *The Phantom Heroine: Ghosts and Gender in Seventeenth-Century Chinese Literature*. Honolulu: University of Hawai'i Press, 2007.

Ziskin, Rochelle. *Sheltering Art: Collecting and Social Identity in Early Eighteenth-Century Paris*. University Park, PA: Pennsylvania State University Press, 2012.